MW00637534

"There's nothing mundane here! Ke·
the wondrous world around us. It's a
lethargic, day-to-day routine. Allow Kevin to guide you to see
what he has seen. You might find that life can be downright
interesting, vibrant and productive once more."

—Max Armstrong, Broadcaster, Chicago, IL

"Kevin will brilliantly uplift and inspire you as you go through
this collection of deep wisdom. You may find that just one story
could change your life in a profoundly positive way."

—Peggy McColl, *Author of The 8 Proven Secrets to SMART Success*

"Reading *Vantagepoints on Learning and Life* is like sitting next
to somebody who is genuinely, thoroughly kind. Someone
patient enough to listen deeply to you and to himself. Someone
honest. Someone fun. Someone you can be quiet with. Someone
very much like a friend."

—Bernie DeKoven, USC School of Cinema Television and
Principal, Deep Fun

VANTAGEPOINTS ON LEARNING AND LIFE

Finding Learning Opportunities
in Everyday Situations

Kevin Eikenberry

Copyright 2006 by Kevin Eikenberry

All rights reserved. This work may not be reproduced, in whole or in part, including illustrations, in any form without written permission from the publishers.

Taken from issues of Vantagepoints, ISSN: 1524-6841

First published by Dog Ear Publishing
4010 W. 86th Street, Ste H
Indianapolis, IN 46268
www.dogearpublishing.net

ISBN: 1-59858-075-2

This book is printed on acid-free paper.

Printed in the United States of America

Dedication

This book is dedicated to everyone who has touched my life and helped me learn the lessons that make me who I am.

Acknowledgements

While there are many I could acknowledge, these people deserve far more than these brief words of thanks.

For my parents, for their example and love.

For Lori, Parker and Kelsey, who you will come to know in these pages, for their support, belief in and patience with me.

For all of my clients and colleagues from whom I have learned so much.

For the Dog Ear team, for their professionalism and help.

For Jenny Pratt whose editing expertise has improved this book immensely.

For everyone else mentioned in the pages that follow, for the lessons they have given me.

And for my team, Holly Powers and Brett Atkin, for their encouragement and effort, without it you wouldn't be holding this book.

Praise for Vantagepoints on Learning and Life

"Lifelong learning is for everyone. Kevin's lessons have two purposes. One—for you to learn from his journey. Two—to inspire you to reflect on, and learn from your own. Read this book for yourself, and create your own success."

—Jeffrey Gitomer, Author of *The Little Red Book of Selling* and *The Sales Bible*

"Wow—reading this is like 'sitting at the foot of a master' and learning about the meaning of life. Thank you, Kevin, for an absolutely terrific book."

—Bob Burg, author *Endless Referrals: Network Your Everyday Contacts into Sales*

"Kevin Eikenberry's gift for leadership manifests itself not only in his business career but also in his voluntary efforts on behalf of his alma mater, Purdue University. His essays reveal him as a keen observer and an intense participant in life. Like all strong leaders, he understands how to communicate his ideas passionately and vividly."

—Martin C. Jischke, President, Purdue University

"I was taught that practice does not make perfect...practice actually makes permanent. Practice something wrong and you will get to be good at doing it the wrong way. This book teaches us that Life is certainly a set of practices. Kevin's honest and touching peek into his own life lessons gives a good sense of how to take the 'everyday' of life, put it into practice in the right way with a sense of discipline, add some heart and soul, and the result is a better human being. That makes this book much more than a book. It is a gift of life from Kevin to us."

—Rusty Rueff, Executive Vice President, Electronic Arts

"There's nothing mundane here! Kevin awakens the reader to the wondrous world around us. It's a great antidote for the dull, lethargic, day-to-day routine. Allow Kevin to guide you to see what he has seen. You might find that life can be downright interesting, vibrant and productive once more."

—Max Armstrong, Broadcaster, Chicago, IL

"Reading *Vantagepoints on Learning and Life* is like sitting next to somebody who is genuinely, thoroughly kind. Someone patient enough to listen deeply to you and to himself. Someone honest. Someone fun. Someone you can be quiet with. Someone very much like a friend."

—Bernie DeKoven, USC School of Cinema Television and Principal, Deep Fun

"I love what Kevin has written! He challenges us to view the simplest aspects of our lives in new and fresh ways. He stretches us as he shares his own everyday insights. I am reminded of a quote I love by William Winter: 'As much of Heaven is visible as we have eyes to see.' Kevin has given us a profound and touching glimpse of our Heaven on Earth, seeing the ordinary as extraordinary and finding a new depth in our existence. Thank you, Kevin, for touching our heads and our hearts!"

—Barbara Glanz, CSP, Speaker, Consultant and Author of *CARE Packages for the Workplace* and *The Simple Truths of Service*

"*Vantagepoints on Learning and Life* is a marvelous exploration into this vastness of everyday life. Strewn all about are lessons that elude us simply because we have never learned to seek after them, appreciate them, and utilize them. Kevin picks up those jewels, polishes them off and holds them up to the light for us to benefit from.

"You hold in your hand far more than words on a printed page. You are now in possession of a precise set of intangible tools that will hone and fine tune your life. Use them well."

—Scott Ski, Author of *Dogged and Determined* and *InCite*

"I think of Kevin Eikenberry as the ANTI-David Copperfield (I know, I know, but hear me out). David Copperfield influences you to see things in such a way as to make the extraordinary disappear. Kevin, through his Vantagepoints, urges you to see ordinary things from an angle that exposes the extraordinary. These new perspectives on seemingly mundane experiences and events are like cerebral breaths of fresh air.

You will find yourself engaging in new and creative processes before you've even finished the book, and like me, you'll be anxious to apply these new perspectives into your career, your family and other personal and professional relationships. One warning, though…your copy of *Vantagepoints on Learning and Life* will quickly become dog-eared from constant revisiting and reference."

—Tracy Forner, Morning Anchor, WXIN Fox 59 Indianapolis

"It is true that in this book Kevin's purpose for writing *Vantagepoints on Learning and Life* comes through loud and clear: Allow life to transform you into a lifelong learner. You already are, and you just may not be aware of it. However what you have in your hands does something else: It challenges you to be a better person, and it has an underlying message that there can be no excuses: you will no longer settle for less. Kevin has shared a collection of stories that are profound in what they can individually mean to each reader. Start reading as soon as you can, and learn about the person you are meant to be. After you have finished, be sure you have a day or two to simply walk outside and let life swallow you up——even better if in the company of those you love, for you will never look at the everyday bliss of life in the same way again."

—Rosa Say, Founder, Say Leadership Coaching and author of *Managing with Aloha*

"*Vantagepoints on Learning and Life* is very easy to read and contains great thought provoking stories. What really sets it apart are the Action Items at the end of each section; those little things for me to try on or think about. My mother always said, 'The Devil is in the Details Hazel, it is the little things that make the difference.' Your book is full of those little things that make a big difference, those little things that we as busy humans forget about. Thanks for the reminders!"

—Hazel M. Walker, Executive Director BNI-Central Indiana

"I've been a subscriber to *Vantagepoints* for many years and find that Kevin always has a valuable message to share. He has the uncanny ability to send the right advice at just the right time. Many thanks Kevin for your insights into ordinary daily life that most of us wouldn't see without your guidance."

—Andrew Grainger, longtime Vantagepoints reader from South Australia

"*Vantagepoints on Learning and Life* inspires you to think about how little things in life have so much meaning. I have read a lot of books about goal setting, motivation and creative learning methods. This book is different from many of the others because it is so compelling you won't want to put it down. It is an adventure to read. I found myself reading on just to see what the next lesson on life will be and how I can apply it to my own life."

—Doug Edge, Executive Director, Entrepreneurs' Alliance of Indiana

"Kevin is quite adept at making the mundane seem less ordinary. His anecdotes, mostly personal, are pleasurable to read because of their 'human-ness.' Each essay has an almost Reader's Digest-like appeal, but is far more real."

—Allison Boxill, longtime Vantagepoints reader

"If you are looking for ways to get brain cells reactivated this is the read for you. This book illustrates the power of relationships in our life, how they affect us positively and negatively. Kevin captures the heart of why life is worth living to our fullest."

—Tony Scelzo, Co-Founder, Rainmakers

"Kevin Eikenberry's *Vantagepoints on Learning and Life* contains what I believe to be a wonderfully inspiring collection of lessons we can all benefit from greatly. The ideas clearly show how to get back to focusing on the amazing details that sometimes end up going unnoticed in our day-to-day lives. This is one book you'll want to keep handy so you can review it often—- practice the ideas in it—- and yes, as a result lead a more inspired life.

—Josh Hinds, http://GetMotivation.com

"Kevin will brilliantly uplift and inspire you as you go through this collection of deep wisdom. You may find that just one story could change your life in a profoundly positive way."

—Peggy McColl, author of *The 8 Proven Secrets to SMART Success*

"Sometimes we all need a good reminder on what is important in business and life. Kevin Eikenberry's *Vantagepoints* are a great learning tool for me to see life's situations in a whole new way and to find valuable insight from all our experiences. I've shared many of the lessons learned with my colleagues and family!"

—Ken Bowman, Manager of Technology, Chevron Products Company

"This book is a wonderful treat. These short gems are perfect for the person who wants to take a few recharging, rewarding minutes out from a day of multi-tasking. Read one a day until you've read them all, then start over. Or indulge yourself and read all of them at once! No matter how or when you choose to open and read this treasure trove, you are going to be enriched by the words and the wisdom."

—Stephanie West Allen, JD, Founding Partner, Allen&Nichols Productions, Inc.

"*Vantagepoints on Learning and Life* is an enlightening example of the powerful habit of learning from life's daily activities and interactions. Kevin Eikenberry's calls to action provide a guide to creating the vital link between this immense opportunity and tangible, personal growth."

—Eric Averitt, Principal, New Perspective Group

"I have heard it said that adults don't need to be taught so much as they need to be reminded of what they already know. Kevin has a wonderful gift for reminding me of what I know but don't always apply. His writing is friendly, inviting, engaging, challenging and encouraging. He gently challenges me to think and live on a higher plane without criticizing or condemning. By revealing his life lessons, he helps me to reflect on and learn from my own experiences. *Vantagepoints on Learning and Life* contains absolute gems from Kevin's impressive collection of essays and articles. I highly encourage you to read, reflect and remember as you experience this work."

—Guy Harris, Chief Relationship Officer, Principle Driven Consulting

"As a teacher, trainer, counselor, coach and parent, I have enjoyed the use of personal stories and metaphor as powerful teaching tools. In this book Kevin stirs up a series of powerful, sensory mixtures to see, hear, smell, feel and taste, as the reader translates the lessons into his/her own life experience."

—Dr. Anita Schamber, Leadership and Organizational Development Team, World Vision International and co-author of *Real World Career Development Strategies That Work* and *Coaching: Evoking Excellence in God's People*!

"Kevin's created a place for reflection in the bustle of the everyday. He holds up his own life experience in a way that allows us to both dig down and step back from our own."

—Michael Bungay Stanier, creator of *Get Unstuck & Get Going...on the stuff that matters*

"Kevin Eikenberry has an unmatchable appetite for learning, and a contagious enthusiasm for…well, just about everything. In this volume, he shares his passion and insights in accessible pieces that offer entertainment in the moment and practical tips and inspiration for much longer."

—Kat Koppett, author of *Training to Imagine*

"Kevin's thoughts and insights are absolutely terrific! This book will help you rediscover the magic in your everyday life. A great diversion for anyone who needs to slow down and get refocused on what's really important in their lives."

—CJ McClanahan, Business Coach

Table of Contents

Forward by Jane Mullikin xviii

Introduction by Kevin Eikenberry .xx

About Commitment 1
Expanding Your Perspective 3
Important Life Lessons...From Darts... 6
Asking Why 9
Secret Samaritans 11
Take Some Time 14
Go Slow to Go Fast 17
Lessons From a Yard Needing Improvement 20
Personal Mastery 23
The Auction 26
Planting Corn 30
Everyone Has Something to Teach 33
Learning From the Past 36
Smile! 39
Working with Passion 42
Hugging for Health 45
A Warm Spring Day 49
The Voice 52
Your Associations 55
Message in the Sand 58

I Have a Hobby 61

Volunteering 63

Deciding and Doing 66

I Wonder Where the Wonder Went 70

Say It 74

Fears of All Sizes 77

I Saw the Light 81

Hello and Goodbye 85

Have Yourself an Awful Little Christmas 88

Reflections of a Sports Fan 93

Thanks! 97

Pretty Please (With Sugar on Top) 101

Passages 105

Slug Bug Black, No Tag Backs 109

The Good Stuff 113

U-Pick 116

Go Tell it on the Mountain 119

And the Wall Came Tumbling Down 124

I'll Take Mine Hand Cranked 128

The Words Do Matter 131

It's Our Choice 134

Better Than a Pot of Gold 138

Short But Not So Sweet 142

The Great Flood 146

Halloween 150

Getting the Right Start 155

Give Me a Break 159

Doing a Happy Dance 162

Heads or Tails 167

What I Learned on My Trip to Margaritaville 170

A Lesson in Leadership 174

Worth the Wait 177

Garage Sale Bargains 181

Let's Play! 185

The Lesson of the Rhubarb Pie .188

They've Got Game 192

Lessons of the First 100 195

About Kevin Eikenberry 199

Our Special Thanks to You 201

Listen to *Vantagepoints* Live 202

About Our Products and Services 203

Foreword

It's the everyday non-event that holds great, life-expanding growth potential. When we allow ourselves to be bombarded with world, national, sports and entertainment events, we are drained before we ever get around to us.

"To put the world right in order, we must first put the nation in order; to put the nation in order, we must first put the family in order; to put the family in order, we must first cultivate our personal life; we must first set our hearts right."
—Confucius

We need to see, feel and act upon the little messages coming to us each day. It is the gentle, easily missed little "lesson" found within those everyday non-events that has the potential to make our hearts right.

When our hearts are right, we will unconsciously deliver the right messages to our children. We can tell them about integrity all day long. We can preach on a set of values. If they, with the uncanny honesty of a child, see our actions in conflict with our words, they will not hear our words.

This book is about a right heart. It is about a family raised up with a right heart. This book is about you and me. It is about helping us see the magical truths delivered through everyday non-events:

As I sit in the sand, I think about how the sand is like life.

Spend some time looking at the stars.

Seeing the wonder in things around us is one of the ways we make our lives more meaningful and enjoyable.

Go slow to go fast.

Ask yourself whose day I could improve by giving a hug today.

While I will acknowledge that Kevin learned much about life through education and experience, I think his family is the real source of his understandings about personal integrity. Many valuable life lessons come early when one is raised in the vast farmlands of Mid-America. There is the awareness of the life cycle through livestock birthing, the understanding that the crops are more dependent on the weather than anything the farmer can control. There is the daily quiet time where nature is one's companion while chores are mindlessly accomplished.

Kevin's lifelong lessons in a right heart, in a love of nature and family started before his earliest memory. With such a foundation, a child is able to stay solid in his values during the developmental years. Kevin is in touch with reality; he is able to cut through the clutter and see the simple realities, pulling life-enhancing lessons from them.

As a longtime reader of Kevin's *Vantagepoints*, I look forward to each one and believe they have brought valuable insights into my life as well as the lives of his audience on my website. He is one of the more popular writers on SpiritualSisters.com, and we look forward to continued insights into the building and maintaining of a right heart through the words of Kevin Eikenberry.

I believe you will enjoy and benefit from the essays that follow as much as I and many others have.

Jane Mullikin
www.spiritualsisters.com and www.hopeandspirit.com

Introduction

Vantagepoints began as a way to communicate with my clients. It began as a way to share what I was learning with one client with others. It was meant as a learning tool, and, yes, as a marketing tool to help me keep my name in the minds of my clients. *Vantagepoints* began before email was prevalent, so it was delivered via fax.

Quickly though, *Vantagepoints* evolved. It continued to contain lessons for our business lives, and many business people continue to receive and benefit from them each month, but it transformed from lessons I was learning in business, to lessons I was learning from my life.

For many people, learning is connected to school. People think about learning in a classroom, in the orientation to a new job, in a training class, in college or in a seminar. Obviously, these are all places that we can learn.

Sadly, too many people think of these places as being the primary place for learning. You see, while we have all spent much time in those settings, the hours spent in those settings pales to the total hours of our lives.

In the movie *The Last Samurai,* Tom Cruise's character says "Every breath is life." It is a beautiful sentiment. I would say "Every breath is learning." Our bodies continue to learn and adapt to our surroundings as a natural part of being human. Our minds and hearts stand ready to learn as well. It is for us to decide to become learning beings and to engage ourselves completely in the learning process.

We can engage ourselves in many ways. We can read more, attend more seminars, go back to college, get a mentor and a thousand other things. I heartily endorse those options. But even in the midst of all of that activity, our life goes on…and if we don't recognize the learning opportunities all around us, and find ways to extract the lessons, we are missing life altering opportunities everyday.

This is the true enduring mission of *Vantagepoints* and of this book. I write these essays to help me reflect, to help me gain understanding, to help me revisit the truest and most important lessons I can learn about being a growing, caring, compassionate, successful and wise human being.

It is my hope that you will enjoy, learn from, and yes, even, take action (gasp!) on what you read on the pages that follow. It is my much greater hope that you use these pages to help you see how *you* can learn more from your everyday life experiences; that you can begin to see that "Every breath is learning."

A final note: Over the years I have written more than 100 of these essays. 56 were selected for this book, by my team and me. They are presented to you in chronological order. Why? Because putting them in some sort of thematic order doesn't mirror how we find new lessons and learning in our lives. Events occur everyday that offer us opportunities to learn—life typically does not follow a theme or pre-defined pattern.

I also have chosen to present these to you in this way because, as a reader you see through this writing how I have grown over the years. It is my hope that this can provide another valuable insight for you too—that our growth never ends, and who we are at the time of an experience helps us create the lessons we find.

Kevin Eikenberry

*Often the greatest truths are seen
in the simplest acts.*

About Commitment

Once you've made that commitment, your chances of success will skyrocket. And so, not inconsequentially, will your enjoyment of the process.

The story goes that the chicken and the pig were passing by the cafe in the early morning watching people ordering their breakfast. The chicken began to boast about how important chickens were—committed to the human population by giving them eggs for their breakfast. The pig quickly laughed, saying while the chickens were involved, the pigs were truly committed by providing the bacon.

Today I'm writing about commitment.

We spent this past Saturday at an amusement park, and it was very hot. Early in the day we sat in a show and (as promised) got a bit wet as we watched—not drenched—more like walking through a brief rain shower. I noticed my three-year-old son complaining about the water—wanting to escape it. However, as we walked out, he spied some of the water hoses and other "getting wet" equipment and decided that he would investigate (apparently forgetting that only a moment before he hadn't wanted to get wet). At first he gingerly walked into the area but quickly bolted out—wanting only a brief encounter with the water. With each attempt, he grew bolder and got a bit wetter.

At this point I'm sure you're wondering what all this has to do with commitment. Actually it has *everything* to do with commitment. At first Parker didn't really want to get wet, he just wanted to investigate, because it seemed that others were having fun. How often do we get involved with a new project, product line, idea or whatever, but don't really give it our all?

We are just "testing the waters." Parker was having a little fun just "testing the waters," but he was pretty inhibited, a bit timid and unsure. How often are we a bit timid or a bit inhibited when trying out the new project, exercise regimen, diet or whatever?

All the time!

Why? Because, like Parker, we aren't yet committed!

Soon Parker had his shirt off, and spent the next 40 minutes playing in the water—in his full glory. When he finished (and all the while he was doing it) he had a huge smile on his face showing his complete and total enjoyment. And while he was playing, getting as wet as you could possibly be, he was teaching his Dad about commitment. Once he decided getting wet was OK, he succeeded. Once he committed, his success was assured.

I believe that is completely true for us too! I'm sure each of you is working on, or thinking about, something today, that you aren't completely committed to. Let me urge you to first make a decision about this issue. Is it something that you believe you should be doing? Is it in alignment with where you want to take your organization, your family or yourself? If so, then commit. Once you've made that commitment, your chances of success will skyrocket. And so, not inconsequentially, will your enjoyment of the process.

Expanding Your Perspective

How often do we get caught up in our own perspective on a situation, getting blinded to other options and/or opportunities?

Friday, it rained. It's Indianapolis, and the weekend of the second annual Brickyard 400 NASCAR race. This is a big deal. Largest purse in the sport. The second day of qualifying was a washout too. Friday night, all the weather forecasts said the likelihood of running was slim as the remnants of Hurricane Erin were on the way.

Friday night, it rained.

Saturday morning, it rained.

People still went to the track for the 12:15 start time. They all got wet, and they all waited. All 300,000 of them. They all wanted it to stop raining. The 41 drivers, their teams, their owners, their sponsors—they all wanted it to stop raining. The track owners. They wanted it to stop raining. The ABC network which was going to televise the race live. They wanted it to stop raining.

It rained anyway.

The rain was the big story here this weekend; most of the stories about how awful it was—potentially ruining the second running of this race. But not everyone was upset...

Somewhere in central Indiana there was a gardener who was glad it rained, because now she would have better tomatoes for canning. There were lots of farmers who were pleased at the rain, as it came at a critical time to the maturation of their corn crop. Lots of suburban home owners were glad too—the rain would keep them from dragging hoses to water their lawns for at least a few days. As it turns out, the food vendors in and around the Speedway also liked the rain, as they could sell more food to the thousands of bored and hungry fans. Somewhere too, a family took the rain as a pleasing Saturday morning excuse to relax, and maybe sleep in.

Same rainstorm.

Very different perspectives.

How often do we get caught up in our own perspective on a situation, getting blinded to other options and/or opportunities? We spend our time saying (or thinking) "Woe is me, the situation is so bad." The reality is that the situation is just a situation, neither inherently good nor bad.

What made the rain "bad" to so many people was perspective. They told themselves it was bad. But inside there was lots of opportunity. How many new friendships were formed because people talked to those around them in their seats during the (four hour) wait? And what will people talk about, in three months or three years about this race? Will it be Dale Earnhardt's pass at the end, or will they laugh about the rain? I think you know the answer.

The rain was neither good nor bad. Neither is the situation facing you right now. It is surely not as completely bad as you might think. Put on a different pair of glasses for a minute.

What other perspective is there that you could consider? And what changes to your plans could you make because of it?

My advice in four words?

Proactively expand your perspective!

Important Life Lessons... From Darts...

We all need to focus to achieve better results—whether leading a team, driving our car, teaching someone something, playing darts or anything else.

Several months ago I found a new hobby—throwing darts. So far I've played mostly while traveling, as something to do instead of TV in a hotel far from home. This past week I was in Orange, Texas, staying at the Ramada Inn—where I started throwing and have played the most. As I played during the week (sometimes quite successfully, and other times, well…I'm getting better) I thought about what darts is teaching me, or reminding me, about living a successful life.

Competition

Those that know me know that I am quite a competitive person. As I grow older, I think I've learned to focus that competitive spirit internally—as a way of pushing and challenging myself. In Orange I've played against some quite accomplished players and have now been able to beat them at least occasionally. Now I expect that I can win—and this internal expectation is making me a better player. The same can be said about anything—if we challenge ourselves to higher levels of achievement, we are taking a positive step towards getting there.

Graciousness

Competitiveness can degenerate into people being "sore losers," or maybe worse, "bad winners." Hopefully my competitiveness can't be described like that very often. I've watched lots of dart games over the last few months—some highly competitive and very close—but most always both winner and loser were gracious at the end of the game. That's always a good lesson for all of us, especially us competitive types.

Focus

As with many things, focus pays when playing darts. Boyd, one of my dart mentors in Orange, often tells me, "Slow down Kevin, you're throwing too fast." Often he isn't even watching the board—only hearing the darts hit the board. Boyd is right. We often try to do too many things at once, or try to finish what we're doing too quickly. Focus. When I focus on doing things right, and aiming at my preferred target, my results improve. Ed, another of my dart cheerleaders, often stops after missing a couple of shots, to step back and walk around. When he returns for the third dart, his results are almost always better. He got his focus back. We all need to focus to achieve better results—whether leading a team, driving our car, teaching someone something, playing darts or anything else. Focus. The advice to "slow down" might speak to you too—it does to me.

Consistency

Throwing darts is like casting a line, shooting free throws or any of a million other physical tasks: you get better when you do things the same way—every time. Put your foot in the same place, hold the barrel the same way, decide where to shoot, focus, follow through. As I do these things consistently my dart game improves. Decide what the critical steps are—decide what works best. Do those things over and over, and over, and your effectiveness will continue to grow. Practice makes better. Perfect (doing those steps consistently correctly) practice makes perfect.

Fun!

I started playing because it was fun. I keep playing because it is fun. Make sure you find time in your life to have fun. Enough said.

Sure, it's a simple game in a neighborhood bar. I've made new friends, gotten better at the game, and reminded myself of some important life lessons. I hope these lessons are useful to you. And to think…you didn't even have to throw a dart.

Asking Why

Curiosity leads to learning, whether we are exploring new things or solving problems. Curiosity is a wonderful thing, something we never need outgrow.

All kids go through *the stage*. It is one of the fabled stages in the growing up process. That time when every statement requires further explanation, every statement is followed by "Why?" Anyone who has been through it won't likely forget it, and while they laugh about it later, there are times when the "why's" become overwhelming and may lead to much frustration (and maybe a "Because I said so!").

I've been thinking a lot about "Why," and wondering why (is it contagious?) all kids seem to go through this stage. I am convinced I have figured out at least part of the reason. "Why" is a very powerful question. It is perhaps the best way to cut through the clutter to better understand a situation. In order to better understand anything, we either ask why or some variation of it.

You may be familiar with a problem solving technique called the Fishbone Diagram. If you're not, it's a technique where a problem statement is placed in the head of the fish and lines are drawn identifying major possible causes of the problem.

(These major areas often include things like: people, machines, materials, processes, etc.) Each of these areas is then explored, trying to determine the root causes of the problem. The thinking is that once we understand the root causes of a problem, we are in a much better position to solve the problem.

All of this is relevant because the best way to use the Fishbone Diagram is to ask "Why?". Let's say you have brown spots in your lawn. Perhaps you think one possible cause is lack of water. To check your hypothesis ask, "Why would there be a lack of water?" The answer might be that it hasn't rained in three weeks. "Why hasn't it rained in three weeks?" You get the idea.

The power of the Fishbone Diagram is the "Why?". If you will ask yourself "Why?" over and over, you will get to the root cause (usually in five why's or less). How will you know you're there? When you can't think of any way to answer your last "Why?". (The end of my earlier example might be that it's July—a month of little rain. "Why is it July?" You can see there's not much hope to pursue that one!)

So back to Parker and his constant asking of "Why?" He asks because he's curious. He wants to know more about the world around him. Curiosity leads to learning, whether we are exploring new things or solving problems. Curiosity is a wonderful thing, something we never need outgrow.

Maybe we all need to start asking "Why?" more often. We may solve some problems, we may learn some things, and maybe we might recapture a glimmer of what it's like to be a kid. Not bad returns for a simple question.

Secret Samaritans

This simple act of helping someone—with no desire (or possibility) of repayment is good for us and our self-image, and it may positively change the life or outlook of the receiver for the day!

I've got something for you to try. The next time you are at a tollbooth, after paying for your toll, pay for the person behind you too! I read this idea several years ago, paying for the next person and asking the toll taker to give them your business card. (Apparently at least one realtor has done very well with this marketing approach.)

I always thought this was an interesting tactic, but had left it at that. Last week, though, as I neared the Bay Bridge, heading towards San Francisco, I was reminded of the idea, by a friend and associate, Leslie Brunker. She said she always pays for the person behind her, anytime she's at a tollbooth. So, that's what I did, I told the toll taker to pay for the next person, and tell them "Happy Valentine's Day." This led to a discussion of Leslie's experiences in doing this, with some great stories of how people respond. During our conversation, the receiver of my dollar, barreled up along side me and waved a thank you.

The entertainment value was worth the dollar, but that is not why I am recommending you try it. I'm recommending it for what it does for the other person. Ever find a quarter on the ground? What happens after finding that twenty five cents? Are you a bit nicer? Are you a bit friendlier? Is their a bit more lightness in your step? I'll bet the answer is yes to at least one of those questions.

There was a study done to look at what is now called the "Good Samaritan Effect." In the study, researchers stood near a pay phone and studied the people who made calls. One of the things they learned was that nearly everyone checked to see if there are any coins in the coin return after placing a call. Think about it, it is nearly irresistible to see if the machine made a mistake and returned your quarter.

This behavior gave the researchers an idea. The next day they randomly placed coins in the coin return slots, so some people did actually discover money. The researchers then had a young woman walk by the phone at the exact moment the people were hanging up. When the woman walked by with her arms full of books, she pretended to stumble and drop them on the ground.

What they learned was that the people who had just found money in the coin return were four times more likely to stop and help the women with her books than were those who didn't find any money. They concluded that when we feel good, we tend to do good.

This simple act of helping someone—with no desire (or possibility) of repayment—is good for us and our self-image, and it may positively change the life or outlook of the receiver for the entire day!

Maybe you don't have a tollbooth near you. But there are other ways to apply this advice.

Pay extra in the parking meter.

Randomly drop coins as you run or jog.

Put a coin in the coin return—pay phone, candy machine, newspaper machine, wherever.

Buy a movie ticket for the next guest who walks up (especially if there is no one in line).

These are just a few. There are many other ways. I'd love to hear what your experiences are with trying this, and what other ways you find to try it.

Try it today—you'll be glad you did!

Take Some Time

However masterful we are in our current situation, we can't move on without learning, without risking, without taking the time.

I am blessed that in my work I very often see people grow and develop new skills in a relatively short period of time. It is a wonderful thing to observe people grow as they discover latent talents and skills they never even know they had.

In every case, before people can learn new skills/talents, they must be willing to change; they must be willing to become learners—beginners—again. Of late there are two particular people I've been thinking a lot about. I have been thinking specifically about their situations and their progress. I'm not going to say who they are, but I am going to talk generally about their situations and how they relate to all of us.

Both of these people have been exposed to new thoughts, ideas, skills, people and experiences over the past several months. Both have great reputations for their work. Both recently have been asked to move into new roles. These new roles are a big departure from their prior work, and these new roles have changed both of their lives. Their lives are changed because of the new experiences, ideas, and mostly, *their response* to the change.

Once we've been someplace new, whether that's through a vacation, a business trip, reading a book, doing a new task, meeting someone new, or whatever, we are never the same person again. All of us intuitively know that this is true.

One of the things that set these two people apart is that they are using these new experiences in a very thoughtful way—to consciously expand themselves and their perceptions of their futures. Both of their minds have been stretched, and they will never again be the same.

All of us have these experiences, but often we don't take full advantage of them.

So, how *do* we take advantage of them? While there are many things you can do, let me share part of what these two people have been doing.

Take Time to Think

In order to readjust our perceptions of the world, or paradigms (including our perceptions of ourselves), we must take the time to think about what is happening and what it means to us. Both of these people have spent/are spending much time thinking about their futures as it relates to what they are learning now.

Take Time to Investigate and Discuss

These people are making opportunities to talk to people who can help them understand the changes and their implications. They also are talking to the important people in their lives about what is changing in their lives. This is critical. If we are changing, those closest to us need to know about those thoughts, ideas, experiences, so they can understand what is going on, and changing, in our lives (and how it may require them to change too).

I'm not suggesting that we all need to change our perceptions of our work, our talents and ourselves today. What I am suggesting is that when you feel the "tug" of personal change, that you take the time to let yourself think about it, investigate it, and to discuss it with others. Listen to that gentle intuitive "tug". Pay attention to it, and learn what you can from it. However masterful we are in our current situation, we can't move on without learning, without risking, without taking the time.

Go Slow to Go Fast

*...we often can improve our results simply by slowing down
and focusing on the process as well as the task.*

G o slow to go fast.

I've been telling people this for several years. The admonishment, for me, began with my work teaching quality improvement at Chevron. In that work we found, to no one's surprise, that people often focus on the task—solving a problem—much more than on the process—understanding its causes (and planning solutions accordingly).

Most of us in western cultures focus easily on solving a problem or removing a barrier. After all, we know what's wrong—so we focus on fixing it. As all of us know from experience, the bias for action (only focusing on the task) often leads to incomplete solutions, solutions that cause more problems (maybe ones worse than the original), solutions that don't solve.

Go slow to go fast.

By taking time to focus on process—how we solve the problem—and working to understand the causes of the problem often we achieve better results. The rub is these steps may seem like they take a lot of time. In the moment, that time is often seen as wasted ("Let's just solve the problem!").

Go slow to go fast.

Several recent events have coalesced to remind me of this saying (yes, I do hear myself telling others in my own voice!). On a flight from Chicago to Oakland recently, I was reading a book and put it down with nearly two hours remaining in the flight. This is very odd behavior for me, especially when I am truly enjoying the book. I put it down because I decided some reflection would make the book more valuable and more enjoyable.

Go slow to go fast.

After I put it down and was contemplating what I had read, the flight attendant came by to pick up empty drinks. She mistakenly thought my Coke was empty. As she quickly started to pick it up, it spilled—almost entirely on me! She certainly didn't intend to spill it, and she was very helpful in my cleanup efforts. The point is, she ended up spending much more time with me than she would've had to if the Coke hadn't spilled.

Go slow to go fast.

A trivial example?

Perhaps.

But often the greatest truths are seen in the simplest acts.

This phrase also is in my consciousness as I work with a colleague to build a workshop on consulting skills. This workshop will feature much time for reflection, personal learning and processing. I'm hoping to impress, through my actions, the importance of processing- the importance of slowing down.

There are examples, large and small, of this advice all around us. Since I started formulating this essay in my mind I've already seen many! (Including my tendency to hand write notes too quickly, which make it hard for the reader to read, which could cause miscommunication, etc.)

I urge you to think about the application of this concept to your life. I am sure you will come to the same conclusion I have—that often we can improve our results simply by slowing down and focusing on the process as well as the task.

When you come to this conclusion, I urge you to pick one task or problem you are working on and apply this advice. Slow down. By focusing on the process you are using to solve the problem you will have more clarity and will avoid mistakes. It may be a bit frustrating, but in the long run it will be time well spent.

Go slow to go fast.

Lessons From A Lawn Needing Improvement

Persistence isn't always about hard work; sometimes it is more about consistent wiggling away at the situation.

I t's July, and time now to begin watering my lawn, which means more time spent walking through it, observing, checking for moisture levels and simply moving the sprinklers. As I walk around my yard, I can't help but pick up rocks, pull weeds and do whatever else I can to improve the overall look of my lawn. (Thanks Dad!)

Picking Up Rocks

The ground was hard (the sprinkler hadn't made it there yet), the rocks were very stubborn and I had no tools—only my fingers. I wasn't going to let those rocks win. I wanted them out of my lawn. I couldn't get my fingers around them so I began to gently wiggle them. They didn't budge at first, but slowly, with more wiggling, they slowly became loose enough for me to get a finger underneath, and soon remove them completely.

Just keep wiggling.

I remember as a kid on the farm moving rocks of a much larger size. I used a tractor with a loader instead of my fingers, but the process was exactly the same. Wiggling a little lead to some success. Consistent and persistent wiggling eventually dislodged the rock completely.

The lesson of the rock is this: Persistence isn't always about hard work; sometimes it is more about consistent wiggling away at the situation. When you think you might not succeed, wiggle a little more. The next wiggle may be the one that lets you get your fingers under the problem or barrier—and when that happens, success is just around the corner.

Those Nasty Wild Carrots

This year I have a new weed. I got rid of a couple other types last year, but this year's weed is wild carrot. You may know this weed—they have a taproot which grows deep and straight. I believe the reason they are called wild carrots is not because of their taste (as far as I know) but the smell. Pull a few of these, and your hand will smell just like a delicious fresh carrot.

If you have ever pulled these weeds you will know that it is difficult to get it all out. (Especially if the soil isn't moist.) Often all you get is the top of the plant, which makes the lawn look better for the time being, but doesn't remove the root cause (sorry, I couldn't resist) of the problem.

If I remove all of the vegetation on the top of the ground, but don't get the root, the plant has plenty of reserve energy stored below the surface to keep growing.

We can learn from the wild carrot too.

Our long-term preparation and positive outlook is that storehouse. Often we will face setbacks—our "tops" will be pulled. If we are well prepared and keep a positive outlook on the situation, we will have the strength to move on, keep growing and succeed in the end.

Keep these two thoughts in mind as you face the coming week—keep wiggling and keep preparing. I promise that more than your garden will benefit.

Personal Mastery

*Pride means keeping pace. Pride in mastery means
getting ahead of the curve.*

I read a phrase in an article a few months ago. That article
has been in my Current File ever since. I keep coming back
to the phrase, and today I decided to write about it. The
phrase is "pride in mastery." The article, by Richard
Koonce titled "How to Prevent Professional Obsolescence,"
mentions this phrase in the context of our work ethic.

I grew up on a farm, and I know what it is like to work
hard. What I know about work ethic comes from my childhood
experiences and observing those around me. One memorable
moment in my life was in the middle of a field doing a very hot
job on a very hot day. My Dad said, "Kevin this is why I'm glad
you are in college. You won't ever have to work with your
back—you can work with your brain instead." My Dad was
right—I had a choice.

But how does this relate to pride in mastery?

I think the connection is clear. It doesn't matter whether
the work we do is with our backs or our brains—the key is to
have pride in our work. My Dad has always had pride in his
work, and I do too. All of this commentary is pretty common—

have pride in your work, yeah, yeah yeah. But the words from Richard Koonce take that pride one step farther …pride in mastery.

Mastery may take pride to a new level for you. It is a challenge that requires learning, commitment and responsibility.

Learning

The world is changing fast—and so is your work. The level of change in information, technique, practice and application is awesome. Dedicate yourself to learning—not to just keep pace—but to move ahead of the crowd. Pride means keeping pace. Pride in mastery means getting ahead of the curve. Find ways to get the information, knowledge and skills you need to move towards mastery.

Commitment

Moving towards mastery will require commitment. Ask yourself how much you value pride in mastery. Your commitment comes from the answer to that question. If the value isn't high enough, this isn't a road to travel.

Responsibility

Pride in mastery requires responsibility.

Responsibility to yourself.

Responsibility to those around you to inform them of how your decision affects your priorities.

Responsibility to others to share your knowledge, skills and expertise with them. (Remember the teacher learns more than the student).

Pride in Mastery. It's a phrase that's been sticking with me for several months. Regardless of the decisions that reflecting on this phrase lead you to, I hope the phrase does stick with you and guide you as it has me.

The Auction

Whatever the circumstances, when we feel self-conscious we aren't able to focus all of our energy and attention on the task or situation at hand.

S elf-consciousness. We've all felt it. I felt it recently.

The Lead In

I was asked to present at a conference at my favorite university (Go Purdue!). About the time my session was to end, a farm auction was to start about an hour away. I had previously been to the auction location to view three items with my Dad, and we determined that perhaps we "needed" them (need may be the wrong word—want is probably more accurate in describing our hobby interest in the items!). The auction was publicized to last not more than 2.5 hours. Given that info, and the way I speculated the items would be sold, and the fact that there was no way I could be there until at least an hour and a half into the auction, I faced a dilemma. If I wanted to bid on these items, I'd have to send someone else.

I sent a member of my team to bid on these items. I had complete faith in him to do this, even though he hadn't seen the items, nor did he have much auction experience. It was clear that if we were going to own these things, Brett would make the purchases.

The Look

I left early in the morning excited to speak at the conference, and I was dressed appropriately. I was wearing a suit and a charcoal gray wool overcoat, as it was a cold morning with a strong wind. I looked good!

When my session ended, the auction had already started. I called Brett on his cell phone to see how it was going and if I had spent any money yet. He told me that it looked like it would be a long while before any of the items I was interested in were going to sell. I asked a few more questions and determined that Brett's assessment was probably right—I might be able to get there in time to participate!

I don't know if you've ever been to a farm auction, but for the most part they take place outdoors, with the equipment arranged so that people can gather around to see what's being sold. As you can imagine the dress code for a farm auction is much different than for presenting at a conference (for good reason, especially on a cold day). Because I never expected to be able to see any of the items sell, I hadn't planned ahead to put a change of clothes in the car. My wool overcoat and polished shoes that had been so appropriate when I got in my car that morning, looked completely out of place when I got out of my car at the auction. I looked goofy!

The Lesson

I was VERY self-conscious! I sent Brett home (while he was happy to do this for me, it clearly wasn't his choice for using his time) and I stayed. For quite awhile as I watched the auction I was very self-conscious, wondering what people were thinking about me, and how different I looked. I observed my reactions and the reactions of others. I found it hard to concentrate. Granted, the task I was involved in didn't require great concentration (except for bidding on three items), but I was distracted by my appearance none-the-less.

As the auction went on (much longer than 2.5 hours), I realized it didn't matter what others thought and that no one had probably thought nearly as much about it as I had! Only then was I able to let go of my self-consciousness. Had I let go of these thoughts sooner I would have enjoyed my experience more and had a more enjoyable day overall.

My session at the conference received high marks and people gained value from it, so that marked a successful day. I bought one of the items at the auction, for less than we were willing to spend, so from that perspective the day also was successful. But the most valuable thing that happened to me that day was reflecting back on my self-consciousness.

I now realize that I am more self-conscious in some situations than I imagined. All of us have situations where we tend to be self-conscious. Maybe clothes or appearance aren't one of yours. Maybe it is something completely different. Whatever the circumstances, when we feel self-conscious we aren't able to focus all of our energy and attention on the task or situation at hand.

The next time you notice a feeling of self-consciousness creeping in, ask yourself:

- Is there is anything I can do to "fix it?"
- How important is the matter I'm self-conscious about?
- Is that matter more important than succeeding in the situation I am in?

Focus on the situation at hand. If there is something you can do to reduce the self-consciousness, great—do it. Otherwise, let it go!

It was a valuable auction—more for what I learned than what I purchased. Most of the time the reason for our self-consciousness says much more about us than about those around us. Once we realize that, it is much easier to let it go and get on with it!

Planting Corn

Just as I had to look all the way across the field and beyond to fix my gaze on my destination in order to reach my goal of straight rows, we too must remain mindful and focused on our ultimate goals, objectives and purpose.

Growing up I spent lots of hours on a tractor, and spring was the intensive time for that activity. As I progressed through high school, I eventually was given what was considered the most important spring job of all—running the planter. From then on, through the springs of my college days, I spent lots of time on a tractor pulling a corn planter. Then…I didn't do it again…until this Memorial Day weekend.

Keep Them Straight

Along with learning to operate and maintain the planter correctly (no small set of tasks themselves), it was always clear that in our family one of the most important parts of planting is having straight rows. While my Dad taught me all of the skills needed, he really focused on teaching me to get the rows straight. I learned that the key to straight rows is to always look far ahead—a gaze just past the end of the tractor hood will ALWAYS lead to crooked rows.

The planting metaphor is clear for our lives. In our lives we deal with lots of day-to-day issues, keeping track of details, managing the daily stuff of life—just like I had to operate the planter correctly and keep checking operations (including looking back as I was driving).

But if you want to reach your goals and objectives, you have to keep your eye looking far ahead. Just as I had to look all the way across the field—and beyond—fixing my gaze on my destination to reach my goal of straight rows, we too must remain mindful and focused on our ultimate goals, objectives and purpose.

This forward gaze allows us to anticipate obstacles and challenges while keeping us aware of our desired endpoint. Alternatively, if we don't look out far enough—our life rows will *always* be crooked.

Using My Subconscious

The first couple of times across the field, I was pretty nervous! I wanted to make sure I got the corn safely in the ground, keep my speed correct, watch for obstacles and most of all—"Keep them straight!" I was consciously thinking about all the steps, processes and tasks.

After awhile I moved into a comfort zone. The years since I had last done the planting melted away. My subconscious took over. When we allow our subconscious to work we improve our performance greatly.

Don't know what I mean? Think about riding a bike before and after you learned. Thinking about driving a car at the start of your learning process (especially when learning to drive one with a manual transmission) compared to now. How different was your performance when learning versus later? Didn't performance improve as concentration on the task lessened?

If so, thank your subconscious!

Now What?

As you finish reading this, take five minutes to reflect on the dual lessons of the corn-planting son. Ask yourself the following questions.

- What is my ultimate objective?
- Am I keeping my eye on that prize, or am I allowing the daily stuff of my life to divert my gaze?
- Do I trust myself to do the tasks I can subconsciously, so I can focus my conscious attention on more important tasks?

Your answers, when applied to your life, will produce a bountiful harvest.

Everyone has Something to Teach

"We can learn something from everyone, and we benefit in many ways when we act on that belief."

When I was in college someone I respected in our community told me that his philosophy was that he could learn something from everyone. I thought a lot about that, and over time it became a part of my life philosophy as well.

It is intuitively obvious that everyone has information and knowledge that I don't have. And it is easy for me to list things that I have learned, or am learning, from those around me. Parker teaches me about whales, Kelsey teaches me about living in the moment, Brett teaches me to slow down and Lori continually teaches me about customer service in the real world. These are people I interact with everyday.

But this philosophy is harder to follow in many other cases.

What about people I don't like? Or don't agree with? Or who look or act differently than me? How well does my philosophy hold up then? I've thought a lot about this, and I've determined that there is an ART to trying to learn from everyone I come into contact with. ART is an acronym…let me explain.

Asking

Reflecting

Thanking

Asking. The first step is to ask myself the pivotal question, "What can I learn from this person?" or "What does this person know that would be helpful for me to know?" In some cases this is just an introspective question for me to consider. In other cases, the person may literally have information that would help me reach my goals, and I need to ask them outright.

Reflecting. Next I need to reflect on the answer to my question. When the person has given me information, this means deciding how I can use this new knowledge. In the more introspective cases, reflecting means thinking about what I've learned, and thinking about how to apply that new information or insight into my life.

Thanking. It is important to let people know you are appreciative of their help. The piece of knowledge they shared may warrant a phone call, a nod, a smile or a thank you note (or more than one of the above). Sometimes the learning comes from someone you never really knew, or have no way of actually thanking. In those cases, I believe you can share your sense of gratitude by sharing the learning with someone else, doing a random act of kindness, or anything else that helps you show your gratitude by making your world (and those in it) a little better place to be.

I encourage you to think about my neighbor's philosophy. Do you believe you can learn something from everyone? If so, how can you make your learning more commonplace?

Consider making an ART of this philosophy. I guarantee that applying this ART, once an hour, once a day or once a month, will make you happier, wiser and bring you closer to your goals.

So, who have you learned from today?

Learning From the Past

*Reducing your negative anxiety level will, in itself,
raise your chances for success.*

This week I started work on a new project with a client. I spent the last day and a half, either reading materials previously foreign (or largely so) to me or attending meetings. There's a lot to learn—new phrases and acronyms, names, roles and responsibilities. Several of the meetings also made clearer what I already knew; there are high expectations on my ability to deliver great results. As I reflected on the learning in front of me, and of the expectations for my performance, I began to feel a bit anxious.

Suddenly it hit me!

I've felt this type of anxiousness before, and strangely at the same time of year. What were those circumstances you ask? The start of each new semester in college. The first day of each class went much the same: get the syllabus, hear the course overview and learn about the schedule for projects, quizzes, tests, etc.

The anxiousness I felt then was exactly like what I faced with my new client: lots of learning to do, high expectations being set, and a short time for the learning and expectations to be met.

Learning From the Past

This insight has helped me lower my anxiousness and put things into perspective more quickly than they might have been otherwise. Looking back at my mostly positive experiences at the beginning of semesters, here's what I am doing in my current situation:

1. Taking a deep breath. This type of mental pause helps me gain better perspective. When the anxiousness grows, I stop and take a deep breath.

2. Thinking of past successes. Thankfully I have had successes both scholastically and in my career, where I have effectively dealt with lots of new learning. When I remember those successes, it builds my confidence that I can do it again.

3. Picking up my pen. When I start laying out a plan, I begin to feel better. My plan includes expectations, roles, content to be mastered, timelines, etc. I use a project approach to the learning challenge.

4. Eating the elephant. The only way to eat an elephant is one bite at a time. My plan should help me identify the specific tasks that need to be done. Once I have a list of tasks, even if it isn't complete, I can begin to eat my elephant—one bite at a time.

"The secret of getting ahead is getting started. The secret of getting started is breaking your complex overwhelming tasks into small manageable tasks, and then starting on the first one."
—Mark Twain

These steps have helped me in the past. I know they can help me again. I'm already proving it today. This project will be a success. I know I have a lot to learn, but that's OK. I wouldn't be happy with my work if I wasn't learning everyday.

Think about how you can successfully deal with the kind of situation I've described. Think about—and possibly apply—the steps listed above. Add to or modify the list based on your experience and success. Reducing your negative anxiety level will, in itself, raise your chances for success. Take the time to think it through.

Follow a plan and have fun.

That's my advice to myself over the next few weeks. And it's my advice to you right now.

Smile!

It is human nature to smile when we are happy, or when things are going well, but did you know how easy it is to just smile regardless of the situation?

Driving down the road last weekend, I had a flashback to about twenty-five years ago. We were on a family vacation, driving to see family in New York and Pennsylvania. Mom and Dad, probably looking for ways to keep their two young kids busy, borrowed a sign about fifteen inches long and three inches high. One side of the sign was painted "Smile" and on the other side was "Thanks!".

The sign got a lot of use on the trip. One of us would hold up the sign, so the car behind us could read "Smile." If they did, we turned the sign over, and they got the reward of "Thanks!".

It was the days before seat belts, and we would often be turned around, pressing the sign to the glass, hoping the following vehicle would see the sign and we could elicit a smile. Or we would try to get passengers as they passed us, pressing the sign up to our windows. The biggest scores came from trucks who would often punctuate their smiles with a blow of their air horns!

These were the memories I pondered as I drove last weekend, everyone else in the car asleep. I wondered if the exercise would build the same kinds of memories for my kids some day as it did for my sister Paula and me. I smiled as I drove, reflecting on those memories for a few more minutes and figured that was about it. But then I couldn't seem to get it out of my mind. I started to realize the sign taught me much more than just giving us a fun way to pass time in the car. It taught me something about human nature, sharing and giving, and the power of a smile—and a thank you.

Smile

Have you ever noticed how much better you feel when you are smiling? Scientists can tell us about real changes in our body chemistry when we are smiling, and most of us have heard about the fact that it takes more muscles to frown than to smile. All of that is interesting, but not as important as the mental and physical feeling we have when we are smiling. It is very powerful.

It is human nature to smile when we are happy or when things are going well, but did you know how easy it is to just smile regardless of the situation? Also do you know how easy it usually is to make someone else smile?

Walking through an airport, or down a hallway where other people are, if you make eye contact and smile, what happens? Invariably people smile back—regardless of how sour they looked before that! You don't even have to say anything, just smile. And what happens to you just for that small effort? You keep smiling long after they pass. And I suspect so do they. They have benefited from your simple act, but you have benefited at least as much or more.

Thanks

The smile lesson is important, but no more so than the flipside, the thanks. Playing this driving game was one of the many ways my parents taught us the importance and value of gratitude, most easily expressed with a simple thank you.

The story goes that a farmer took some of his corn to the State Fair and won the blue ribbon, for the best corn. A reporter asked him what he was going to do with the prized ears of grain he was holding. He said he would share the seed with his neighbors. The reporter was visibly surprised and asked, "Why would you want to do that?" The farmer calmly answered that his corn was only as good as his neighbors. "Why sir," said the farmer, "Didn't you know? The wind picks up pollen from the ripening corn and swirls it from field to field. If my neighbors grow inferior corn, cross-pollination will steadily degrade the quality of my corn. If I am to grow good corn, I must help my neighbors grow good corn."

So it is with smiling—and thanking. You are the wind. You can produce smiling faces by spreading your pollen. The cost to you is small, but the fruits of your pollen will be felt all around.

So who are you going to smile at today? (Right now?)

Smile.

Thanks!

Working with Passion

*When you find work that you are passionate about,
miracles can occur.*

Last week I attended the annual conference of an organization (the North American Simulation and Gaming Association—NASAGA.org). I have served on the NASAGA Board for the past six years. During that time I have served as the Chair twice and our company also has produced the annual conference.

Never have I learned as much about myself at one of these conferences as I did last week. One of the things that was made so clear to me last week—by the people, surroundings, and events of the conference—was the power of passion at work.

I observed the passion with which many of the presenters and session leaders worked. It showed in their faces and work and, maybe more importantly, in the results they achieved in helping others learn more about their area of expertise. I observed the passion of the collective community of participants to seemingly never tire through a long conference program each day—with smiles and new friends and new ideas for their work.

The conference was held near one of my clients, so I spent part of one day working with that team. I arrived on the client site ready to work, but dressed differently than usual. I was wearing a tie—a sight increasingly out-of-place in this strictly business casual organization. They asked why I was SO over-dressed.

My wardrobe led to a brief conversation, as I was ready to leave. I was sharing some about the conference with two of my clients. They could see the excitement in my voice and body language—it was clear to them that I was enjoying this confer-ence a great deal. As I started to leave the office, one of them said, "Kevin, you are having too much fun."

I paused just outside the door then turned around and said. "That is the way work is supposed to be. When you love the work you do, it *is* fun."

My comment made an impact, but I didn't think too much more about it. The following day at our banquet, I was given a surprise honor for my service to the organization, and I told this quick story as I said thank you. What I didn't do was finish the story for those at the banquet that night. Maybe they got it; maybe they didn't. Maybe I didn't even get it at the time.

The rest of the story is that having fun in your work comes from passion. When you find that passion, you are duty bound to share it. My work for NASAGA never took all of my time, and there were certainly weeks when I never did more than 30 minutes work for the organization. But what drew me to be involved was a passion for my work that is represented well in this organization and at its conferences.

Having been drawn in, by all accounts, I did a good job of helping the organization move forward. (At least many people said lots of nice things to me during the conference.) I typically responded with "Thanks, but I was just doing my job."

Just doing your job is one thing. Just doing a job you are

passionate about is quite another, and that is what I learned, or re-learned or became clearer about, last week. When you find work that you are passionate about, miracles can occur.

I am now working on how I can live more closely in alignment with those things I am most passionate about more of the time. Last week gave me ample proof of the power and energy and results that can be created by doing that.

So where are you? What is your passion? Are you finding ways to express it and share it with others? If not, why not?

When was the last time you felt true joy and passion in your work? If you can't answer that question quickly, I urge you to think about how you can find that experience again (or for the first time).

Don't delay—do it today. Find ways to express your life passions in your life and work. You will benefit, but even more so will you serve those around you.

Hugging for Health

Hugging is a way of connecting with others, of showing your genuine affection and appreciation, of valuing others and of giving.

I t seems today is the day I need to write about this topic. Consider the following events.

For our business holiday card I have a tradition of sending a thought-provoking story or anecdote along with the card. This year's story was about a woman, her letters to U.S. Servicemen during the Gulf War, and the simple act of sending them a photocopy of a yellow paperclip in her hand. She said the picture represented a hug that she couldn't deliver across the miles. I included a yellow paper clip with each copy of this letter.

At Christmas, in our house, there is lots of hugging. I am not too macho to say that at age thirty-seven the first thing I want to do when I see my Father is to hug him. (Mom too, but that seems more "normal" in our sometimes counter-productive, western civilization.)

My daughter is now seventeen months old. One of the words she now understands is hug. If I ask her to hug her

Grandma, she'll do it. More importantly (to me), if I say, "Come hug Daddy" she will happily do that too. I've noticed in the past few days how completely alive I feel when she is hugging me, regardless of what is on my mind, positive or troubling, prior to the hug. Her hug changes my world.

This morning before I left for a business trip my seven-year-old son got up early to say goodbye to me. The best part of this goodbye was a big hug—initiated by him.

This morning I re-heard, on a tape a fact about hugging. The speaker said most people get far too few hugs each day. The research cited on this tape said we need eight hugs a day for maintenance and twelve a day for growth.

All of this leads me to write about hugs today. I like to hug. I believe in hugs, largely because that's how I was brought up. I hug in the workplace. I hug clients and peers, and I hug at conferences. Over the past few years, with all of the focus on sexual harassment, it has sometimes caused me to pause and wonder if my hugs are "unwelcomed" and therefore a problem. I hope being conscious of the potential problem has made me more careful and kept me from any misunderstandings. On the other hand, I'm pleased to say that I still hug.

Some Suggestions

Hugging is a way of connecting with others, of showing your genuine affection and appreciation, of valuing others and of giving. All of these are positive, healthy, life-enhancing purposes. While hugging is natural and we all know how to do it, I have put together some guidelines to help make you a better hugger.

Begin the hug with great eye contact. This communicates to the receiver the spirit in which the hug is being given.

Be present during the hug. Even if the hug is only for three seconds, devote your total energy and focus on the person you are hugging—even if it's *just* three seconds. Feel how good it is to both give and receive.

When you finish the hug and are pulling away, make great eye contact again. This further blesses the receiver and communicates a positive feeling to them.

A hug is not an opportunity to burp the other person! Be gentle. This goes especially for the guys—remember a hug isn't the start of a wrestling match either.

Avoid the one-hip hug and/or the tee-pee hug. If you are going to hug, do it right! This isn't an excuse to make the hug overtly sexual either, it just makes the hug work.

If you are much taller than the other person, bend your knees. Make the hug comfortable and a blessing.

If you are hugging children, get on your knees and be at their eye level. If they are small enough, pick them up to hug them.

All of these guidelines are about making the hug a completely positive, giving experience. As in many other things in our lives, when we think about others, we can make better decisions. The same is true for hugs—hug with the huggee in mind!

Next Steps

Take a few minutes today to think about how often you give and receive hugs. Remind yourself how it feels to be the receiver of a really good hug—how it can improve your outlook and general emotional state. Do you get your RDR (Recommended Daily Requirement) of hugs each day? If not, why not? Ask yourself whose day you could improve by giving them one or more hugs today.

Your answers to these questions will tell you what to do. The guidelines in this article may help you if you are a bit out-of-practice. But please, for your own benefit, and those you care about, hug someone today.

"I will not play Tug O' War,
I'd rather play Hug O' War;
Where everyone hugs, instead of tugs,
And everyone giggles and rolls on the rug.
Where everyone kisses,
and everyone grins;
everyone cuddles,
and everyone wins."

—*Shel Silverstein*

Note—You can read the full story of the lady and her letters to Servicemen and women at http://kevineikenberry.com/paperclip.htm.

A Warm Spring Day

*When your environment triggers positive memories, take the
time to reflect on and enjoy those memories.*

February 23, 2000. Indianapolis, Indiana. It is sunny and
65 degrees—a truly beautiful day. (It's especially beautiful when you know that our average high temperature is
41 degrees on February 23.)

The day brought back fond memories of warm spring days
in my past. While I don't know the dates, I can label them: "The
first really warm day of spring." Just saying it makes my mouth
turn to a smile and my heart sing!

When I was about 10 we had a day like this. I got off the
school bus and went to the barn to play basketball—without a
coat! There were puddles on the concrete from snow that had
melted off of tractors and trucks, but it didn't matter. Those
puddles became imaginary defenders for me to negotiate
around. Shots were shot—and if I misjudged the rebound, puddles were splashed. I left the barn a mess, but I was happy and
knowing how close spring was.

A warm spring day reminds me of disking a field in front of

my Dad on the corn planter. It gets me thinking of smelling the smells of freshly turned soil, tasting that same dirt on my lips, feeling the sun on my face and thinking of the promises of summer. Summer—all days as warm as this, no classes and a green, growing crop.

At college the first warm day is an amazing thing. Coats are gone! Shorts (or less) are on! On this first warm day of spring, the girls become girls again (and I'm sure the girls remember the same of the boys)! I remember walking and driving around with my friends, "enjoying the scenery…"

All of these are good memories. All of these thoughts came to my mind on February 23rd. On this February 23rd, I had some unexpected news that surprised me, rocked my future just a little and left me a bit emotionally confused. I was having some trouble mentally getting past this short-term thing, when I realized how beautiful it was outside. I realized what I needed to do to help me get out of my funk—I needed to be outside. So I put my work away, and went to the park to shoot baskets—and avoid puddles.

For 40 minutes I ran and jumped and shot, and thought about warm spring days and the happenings of my day.

The sun and the baskets helped my perspective, which was good. But in the days that have passed since I wrote the beginning of this story I've thought about how I could use this experience. There are two things I've learned from this experience:

- When your environment triggers positive memories, take the time to reflect on and enjoy those memories. In many cases they may be therapeutic and helpful. (Hey, it might even give you something to write about!) Take the time for this reflection.

- When something unexpected happens, take the chance to assess its effects in a new environment. I went outdoors. For you it might mean going to a different office, a conference room, home or a park bench. Let a change of environment help you with your mental processing.

The first warm day of spring may not hold a special place in your heart. But many other things probably do. Perhaps it's Memorial Day, or St. Patrick's Day, or a Mardi Gras celebration, or any of a million other things. The event or day doesn't matter. What matters is taking the time to revel in those memories, and if possible, find a way to have those memories help you with a current obstacle.

The Voice

We all are tapped into this spiritual power—and hearing The Voice is one proof of that. To me the question isn't whether we hear the Voice, it is whether or not we listen.

Whether you've seen the movie *Field of Dreams* or not, you know what I mean when I say, "The Voice." I believe all of us have heard a voice, perhaps "The Voice." The Voice may or may not have sounded like the one in *Field of Dreams*. It may have been a voice we recognized; it may have been a family member, it may have been a woman or it may have been a total stranger, but we have all heard The Voice. *Field of Dreams* is a movie about many things: baseball, dreams, family and more. None are more important to me than The Voice.

The first time the movie was on network television I heard The Voice. My grandparents were soon having a 50th wedding anniversary celebration and the family had asked that no one bring gifts. Since gifts weren't expected or requested, I hadn't thought much about giving them anything.

The Voice told me to go write them a letter.

Now.

At 11 p.m. on a Sunday night, when I had to get up early

to go to work, I went in and wrote the first draft of a letter that I ended up reading to them at their party in front of many family members and friends. It was a way to show my love for them, by telling them how my life is different because of them.

Following The Voice in this instance wasn't especially hard nor did it lead to the kind of changes that Ray Kinsella's Voice did (Ray was the character in *Field of Dreams* who built a baseball diamond in his cornfield because of his Voice), but it was important for my growth, and in the end, valuable to my Grandparents.

When we hear The Voice, I believe it is always for the greater good, even if it doesn't seem as such at first. Listening to, and taking action on, The Voice's words is a habit, and when The Voice gives us easy tasks like writing a letter it is an opportunity to practice our listening skills.

Townsfolk and family members declared Ray crazy for doing something that seemed exceedingly crazy to them! He was laughed at and rebuked in his community and came within hours of losing his farm, his business and his home. Ray had every reason not to listen to the Voice. And many times so do we.

Our history books are full of people who heard The Voice, listened and acted. Martin Luther King, Jr., The Disciples of Jesus, the Founding Fathers of the United States, Gandhi, Mother Theresa, Christopher Columbus, Florence Nightingale—these people, with their faults and foibles, all heard and listened to the Voice and made our world a better place. As important as these famous people and their actions are, the people you know—either in your community or your household—who have listened to The Voice to help themselves and others around them are just as instructive.

Much like Ray, picturing the ball diamond in his cornfield, we hear a voice, or see the vision, but we don't listen, we don't act. Usually the voice I hear is clearer than Ray's was—I've been lucky. But that doesn't mean the choices are easy, or the outcomes assured. There have been times I have listened, and times when I haven't. Often when I haven't listened, The Voice became more persistent—forcing me to listen and continually urging me to act.

Your spiritual background and beliefs may give you a name for the Voice. You may call it God's Voice, Allah's Voice, your inner knower, your Mom, your conscience or something else. No matter the name, we all are tapped into this spiritual power—and hearing The Voice is one proof of that. To me the question isn't whether we hear the Voice, it is whether or not we listen.

"If you build it he will come."

"Ease His pain."

"Go the Distance."

These are the words The Voice said during *Field of Dreams*. The movie, through its story, gives us the answers to these initially puzzling requests. The question the movie doesn't answer is, "What words am I hearing, and what am I doing about it?" and "What is my field of dreams?"

Questions worth asking and answering.

Here's to you finding *your* field of dreams.

Your Associations

"Look carefully at the closest associations in your life, for that is the direction you are heading."

Take a minute—right now—to make a list of the people you have associated with—personally and professionally—over the last month. (The list is longer than you think—take your time…)

Now take a look at that list. What patterns do you see? How does this list compare to a list that you might have created a year ago? Who has come and gone? Why? For the people that have joined the list, how are they similar or different from those who left the list?

It's been said that the only differences between us today and ourselves three years from now will be the people we meet and the books we read. (I would add the TV we watch…) It is in this context that I ask you to examine your associations. Perhaps a future message will discuss what we watch, listen to and read, but this one is just about our associations.

As I look at some of the changes in my business and personal relationships over the past few months, it is clear to me that those changes relate directly to changes (conscious and serendipitous) in with whom I am associating. I find myself spending more time talking with, and confiding in, people who believe in my big dreams and ideas. People who are supportive of my plans and objectives. These associations are making a big impact on my life!

Now back to your list…

Look at each person on your list and ask yourself what do they bring to you in terms of you reaching your goals and aspirations. No, I'm not suggesting that you look at your relationships only in terms of what people can do for you. What I am suggesting is that you identify what you are getting from the relationship. There may be many positive things you receive from that relationship, including:

- Love
- Support
- Information
- Camaraderie and friendship

You may also find that you are getting other things, like:

- Negativity
- Non-support
- Focus solely on fun
- Lack of seriousness

or many other things (in either category).

It is important that we examine our relationships because they show us where we are headed. Your list may show that you are on the right track, or that there are people you might want to spend less (or no) time with in the future. Examining your list might lead you to seek out other people to be in your circle of friends.

Thinking about this is only important if you care where you are heading.

Message in the Sand

Ideas become powerful when many people believe and apply them. People become powerful when they band together in a common cause. Individually they may not be able to make a huge difference, but when one becomes ten becomes ten thousand, the power is obvious.

The sun is in my face, a gentle breeze at my back. As I look to the water I see my family playing in the 'surf' of Lake Michigan. I am on a beach with the greatest sand I've ever seen or experienced. It just so happens that this sand is where I grew up—in Mason County, Michigan. The scene is nearly perfect; my family laughing and playing, in great conditions, in a beautiful place.

As I sit on the beach I think about the sand. Sand from nearby was once used to make automobile glass. This sand defines this community in the summer—this beach and the Lake provide a constant stream of vacationers...and revenue. However, my thoughts of the sand are different, more metaphorical...

As I sit in the sand, I think about how the sand is like life.

The sand is always shifting, driven by the wind. In a small area, it seems to change rapidly—dig a small hole and watch how quickly it is erased by the wind. But look at the whole beach and the sand seems to not change at all.

So it is with our lives.

While things change everyday, sometimes with frightening speed, in the big picture, the world doesn't change that quickly—people are still people and their reactions to situations are the same. History does tend to repeat itself, even if the circumstances seem different. Small changes seem fast, but the big picture changes more slowly—like the beach as a whole.

The sand is powerful in large amounts. If I bury my foot in the sand, it is difficult to remove; yet each individual grain is so small it is barely seen or noticed on its own. The sand is powerful in large amounts.

Ideas become powerful when many people believe and apply them. People become powerful when they band together in a common cause. Individually we may not be able to make a huge difference, but when one becomes ten becomes ten thousand, the power is obvious.

My son and I built a pyramid made of sand. Much like a goal, it took time to build and tend it. And much like a goal, when the tending stopped, forces deteriorated the pyramid. Wind, waves and even people's feet reduced the pyramid to a mere memory.

Our goals are much the same. Many people may act as the wind and water, tearing at our goals, downplaying them as "pie-in-the-sky" or "crazy." If we don't tend them, work on them, believe in them, they will crumble or become less than they once were. We must be diligent in maintaining and nurturing our goals, just as we must mend our sand castles if we want them to remain strong and effective.

A beach is a wonderful place, able to provide many memories. A beach, I found, also is a place that helps me reflect on life and myself. I encourage you to go to a beach soon. Put your feet in the sand. Enjoy the warmth and comfort it provides. And think about how your life is like the sand.

That trip to the beach will be a double blessing for you.

I Have a Hobby

Many people don't find great passion in their work. It is important for those folks to find passion in other parts of their lives, and hobbies are a great way to do that.

I have a hobby. Most people I know call it strange or odd. I've only had this hobby for a little more than two years, but it has become important to me for at least three reasons.

First, it is a hobby that connects me to my kidhood. I had a wonderful growing up, and this hobby grounds me in my learning from that important time in my life.

Second, this hobby has allowed me to be a learner again. When I started out I didn't know very much at all about this topic! I have learned about American history, mechanical engineering, marketing, business history as well as things more directly related to the hobby itself. I have had a chance to examine how I learn, when I learn and how I can learn more effectively. (As a trainer and consultant, this is pretty important stuff in itself!)

Third, this hobby has given my father and I an opportunity to deepen our relationship. We have always had a good relationship, but this hobby is something we now share, talk about, scheme and plan about and more.

My hobby you ask?

I collect antique tractors. Not the toys (well OK, I collect those too), but real-life, full-sized, working tractors. Dad and I own seven together, and I own two on my own (for the record, all but one are John Deeres).

But, this article isn't about antique tractors (I'm sure you are glad to hear that!). Rather, it is about hobbies and their importance in our lives.

Many people don't find great passion in their work. It is important for those folks to find passion in other parts of their lives, and hobbies are a great way to do that. Others are fortunate to have vocations that are their avocations as well. Hobbies are equally important to those people to help bring balance to their lives.

Where do you find a hobby? Opportunities are all around us! Think about things you enjoyed as a kid, or things you did then that you wish you could do again. Participating in a sport? Playing a musical instrument? Making something? Collecting something? The possibilities are nearly endless. The best hobbies will come from within, so take some time to let yourself explore and find one that feels right and lifts your spirit.

Hobbies bring us many benefits. Perhaps the benefits I have found may resonate with you as well: improved family relationships, finding value in learning, connecting yourself with an important part of yourself. Your benefits may be different. That's OK. I bet few who read this will pick up the same hobbies. That's OK too. All that *is* important is having a hobby, or finding a new one.

Allow yourself the time to think about this message. You may be saying you have too much to do already and you can't fit a hobby in. I know, I've said it and I've heard it. Think about it though, think about the benefits you will receive, and remember the enjoyment of the effort.

And if you have a tractor to sell, let me know.

Volunteering

One of the most wonderful truths in our world is that when we give of ourselves, we receive blessings back.

During November and December, we often see evidence of it on television, in the newspaper, around town and perhaps in our own memories. Examples of volunteering. Volunteering to help those in need. Volunteering for causes people believe in. Volunteering just to help. Volunteering.

Here are some recent examples I've experienced:

A couple weeks before Thanksgiving, I was leading a session for Red Cross volunteers from across Missouri. I was struck by their commitment of talent, time and energy.

On Thanksgiving Day the local news ran interviews of people who were volunteering their holiday to prepare and serve meals to those less fortunate. I was moved by the story and the reasons volunteers gave for choosing to spend their day in this way.

One evening last week our doorbell rang and when I opened the door, I saw two bags; one holding sand, the other holding white paper bags and small candles. The deliverer was hopping into his truck as I said thanks. He called back, "Luminaries on Sunday night at 6:00 p.m.—everything you need is inside the bags."

All of these are examples of volunteering.

There are as many reasons why people volunteer as there are people and opportunities to do so. These acts got me thinking about volunteerism and reflecting on when I volunteer and why.

An Email Gift and Lesson

Someone I don't know recently did something very nice for me. Her act was described to me through email. As I replied in thanks, I asked for her mailing address—I explained that I wanted to send a more tangible gift of thanks for her kindness and thoughtfulness. Since I did not know this person, I mentioned in the email that if she didn't want to share her mailing address, I understood that as well.

In her response she said she had thought long and hard about whether to give me the address, as she didn't feel it was necessary to receive anything for her actions. She went on to explain that she eventually decided that while she didn't desire anything else, she didn't want to deny me the blessings of giving.

The Blessings of Giving

One of the most wonderful truths in our world is that when we give of ourselves, we receive blessings back.

The people who give their time to support the Red Cross, be it for blood banks or disaster relief, provide a tremendous service. The people serving meals in downtown Indianapolis on Thanksgiving Day are benefiting many. My neighbor who distributed the luminary materials helped many of us smile last Sunday night. The subjects of the volunteering benefited greatly (the real reason we volunteer), but so did those who were volunteering—they received the blessings of giving (the magical outcome of our giving).

This then, is my challenge to you. Think about how and when you have volunteered. What benefits have been gained from those you are serving? In what areas of your life or experience do you feel drawn to help?

While the joy in our hearts may make it easy to think about volunteering now, during the holiday season, the decision to act is one thing, the action is something else entirely. Think about how you can benefit your world in the coming months. Bottle the emotion and good will in your heart and mind now, and release that positive energy in action soon!

Remember that your efforts will benefit others, but you will receive great benefits as well.

Deciding and Doing

There is a big difference between deciding and doing.
The difference is action.

Five frogs sitting on a log.

Four decide to jump off.

How many are left?

Five.

There is a big difference between deciding and doing.

I've heard and read this riddle several times over the past few weeks. I don't know who to attribute it to, but it speaks one of the greatest truths in our lives. There is a big difference between deciding and doing.

The difference is action.

Isaac Newton gave us this truth from a scientific standpoint. "A body at rest stays at rest until a force acts upon it."

Imagine sitting in your favorite spot in your favorite room watching some television. You decide you are thirsty, but you don't get up to get a glass of water. Until you act, you will still be thirsty. Until you apply some force (action) to a body, nothing will happen. You are the force.

Your neighbor often speaks about how much she'd love to quit her job and pursue her craft hobby full time. You encourage her, and help her think through the decision. But five years later, she still has the job she hates. Until she commits, her crafts beautify only the lives of those right around her.

I'd really like to be able to swim. I tell myself "I could save myself if I had to," but I know that is probably wishful thinking. I know if I learned I would have a pleasant way to exercise and a great way to cool off in the summer. Until I take a lesson, I'll be in the shallow end of the pool.

There's a big difference between deciding and doing.

What Action Gives Us

Taking action gives us many things. First we get off our log—we get results. Second we have confidence in our jumping ability for the future. Third, we can see progress towards wherever we are heading. Fourth, depending on the results of our action, we have learning—we learn something about where to jump and how to jump next time.

"We just need to get off to a good start," says the coach. In sports, great comebacks are borne of this. Basketball announcers talk of this at the start of second halves when one team is far behind. They say, "The first five minutes of the second half will tell us about the rest of the game." In other words, if the team that is behind can make some progress, can gain some momentum, then things might change.

How does momentum develop? Mostly from a positive first

step, followed by another, and then another. Momentum is another important thing we gain from action.

Have you ever been asked to give a presentation and noticed that once you got going it got easier? Or noticed how much easier it is to balance a bike once you get going? This is momentum at work. Momentum emanates from action.

So here is a formula for jumping off *your* log.

- Have a dream.
- Make a plan.
- Decide to do it.
- Take a first step.

If you have a good plan, you'll know what the first step should be. But until you take action, you'll forever be on your log. The dream gives us purpose and direction for our action. A plan prepares us and helps us determine which actions to take when. Deciding is a commitment to start, but none of it matters, no results will occur, until we act.

The Good News About Action

Here's another riddle for you:

What's the best way to eat an elephant?

One bite at a time.

This riddle continues the wisdom of the first. Doing often is done in small steps. Remember the ball game? Coming back from 20 down happens one basket at a time. The initial steps we take needn't be big. But they must be taken. One bite at a time. One step at a time. Inch by inch, anything's a cinch.

"The greatest endeavors begin with a first step." This wisdom has been attributed to many people. The *action* is the part of the equation that can't be left out. Take those first steps, act on your dream, and get the results you want.

There is a big difference between deciding and doing.

The difference is action.

It's time to jump off the log.

I Wonder Where the Wonder Went

Seeing the wonder in things around us is one of the ways we make our lives more meaningful and enjoyable…The key is to add more wonder to life by re-capturing past wonder and finding new wonder in the things we do each day.

I was a fifth grader the first time I flew on a commercial plane flight I remember being amazed that I could get all the soft drinks I wanted for free. I remember the wonder of looking out at the clouds and the topography far below. I remember watching us land. The entire thing was a great adventure, and I was full of wonder.

In college I flew once in awhile, and I always got a window seat—I wanted to be able to watch the ground pass below me. The wonderment of it all—the patterns and beauty of looking out the window was overwhelming. Yes, I would sometimes read or do something else, but much of the flight I would sit…and stare…and be in wonder of it all.

Soon after I started working, I found myself flying a bit more, and it quickly became clear that during my business life I would fly—a lot. I mentioned once to my Mom, who loves to fly, that I'd never lose that great feeling that an airplane flight brings—and that I would always get window seats.

Somewhere between flying once every couple months and flying 100,000 miles per year, I moved to the aisle, and I lost the wonder of it all.

Last week, I was booked in a window seat, and I stopped working or reading long enough to spend some time looking out the window. Today, as I write this, I have just finished 20 minutes of window gazing. Some of the wonder is back!

There are many things in our lives that we once considered wonderful (full of wonder). Many of those things we now take for granted. All of this makes me wonder where the wonder has gone.

Where's the Wonder?

I believe seeing the wonder in things around us is one of the ways we make our lives more meaningful and enjoyable. This is one of the reasons we go on vacations. Yes, some vacations consist of little more than a beach (which can be wonderful in many ways), but many take time to learn new things on vacations, going to museums, art galleries or national parks. Some travel to exotic places to marvel at sites, cultures and foods. Wonder plays a big part in the allure of these trips and the satisfaction gained from the experiences.

You may be thinking, is wonder really such a big deal?

Yes!

Why? Think about it; the absence of wonder is often called boredom, or worse, cynicism. These hopefully are not things people aspire to!

Certainly, we all can experience wonder in new things— new locations, new experiences, new books, new ideas—but I believe I found an important key to a more enjoyable life just waiting outside the plane window. That key is adding more wonder to life by re-capturing past wonder *and* finding new wonder in the things I do each day.

Re-discovering Wonder

There are several things we can do to add to the wonder in our lives—to make our lives more wonder-full.

1. Look at things through fresh eyes. Think about things that have become habit for you. The next time you do them, do them as if you were a beginner again. Start with your drive or commute to work. Make it an exercise in finding wonder. For example, perhaps you go by a school on your way. Spend some time thinking about wonderful things from your childhood days in school. Then try this "fresh-eyed" approach to other routine tasks.

2. Make a list of things you found wonderful at different stages in your life. If you write a journal do it there. If not, make your list instead of watching TV one evening. Once you have it, spend some time reveling in the wonders on your list. Think too about how you could re-experience those things again.

3. Take a list of the wonders you find each day or week. Again, a great journaling task or a great routine to add to your planning for a new week.

4. Plan a mini-vacation or a day trip to someplace wonderful for you. I grew up on a farm, so a drive in the country in spring or fall is particularly helpful in restoring my sense of wonder in the growing process. Others might find your mini day to be boring—help them see *your* wonder—and in turn you will experience your own at a deeper level. Then go with them

when they try to recapture their own.

5. Go to an old event and focus on different things. The next time you go to a ball game, focus less on the action and more on the spectators, or vice versa. Go shopping and shop for something entirely different than you usually would. You get the idea.

These are just a few ideas to help you re-infuse your life with wonder. This idea is really taking hold in my life and each day is more wonder-full and more meaningful as well. I believe when you choose to rediscover your wonder, you'll benefit in the same ways.

You know, the Mississippi River is an awesome sight from 31,000 feet.

Say It

"It may go without saying, but it shouldn't go unsaid."
—Doug Patterson

Aunt Verna was more like a grandmother than a great-aunt. You see, Mom's Mom, my grandmother, died when I was still a baby. Mom says Aunt Verna became the closest thing to a Mother I had after Mom died. I have many memories of Aunt Verna and her late husband Wilbur. I remember going to their home, eating well, enjoying fellowship and feeling love there. There has never been a doubt in my mind that my Aunt Verna loves me.

Several weeks ago, I stood over my Great-Aunt's bed seeing her alive for what would be the final time. The last thing she said to me was "I love you." I can't honestly remember if she ever actually told me that before, but I can tell you these words will be my most powerful and lasting memory of her.

I was sitting in a restaurant with an old friend and we were talking about our families, raising our children and life in general. Doug has one son who lives very close to him and another younger son who lives a plane flight away. I asked how his relationship with John (the plane flight away son) was going and he said very well. He said even when there are rough spots in their relationship, John knows when they see each other the first thing his Dad will do is hug him and tell him he loves him.

He went on to say that the same routine plays out when they say goodbye and on the phone (minus the hug). Then Doug made the statement that gave me goose bumps because it so beautifully describes one of my life beliefs. He said, "You see Kevin, it may go without saying, but it shouldn't go unsaid."

Other Experiences

Many years ago I had the opportunity to first take, and then assist with, the Dale Carnegie course. Part of the program is that every week of the fourteen-week program each participant gives a short speech. Those speeches become more honest, more personal and more emotional as the weeks pass. Both in the group I participated in and in the groups I assisted with this lesson came through loud and clear. People spoke of others in their lives they never told they loved or never heard those words from. Some of those speakers spoke of those who had already passed away. Other spoke of people still alive. The regret from each was real. Some still had time to make amends.

Away From Home

The examples I have shared all are about close friends or family relationships. While the application of this truth may have the most meaning in those areas of your life, applying the lesson to your closest personal relationships may not be your challenge. Your challenge may be at work. Hopefully you work with people who you trust implicitly, believe in totally and value greatly. Maybe you assume they know how you feel. Maybe they do; maybe they don't. Either way, the message of this essay is clear.

"It may go without saying, but it shouldn't go unsaid."

Think about how the message applies to you with family, friends, peers, employees—everyone in your life.

Everywhere

Your message may be "I love you." It may be "I trust you." It may be "I honor your commitment." It may be nearly any authentic, affirming statement you assume the other person knows. Sometimes they do know. But even when we know, we still need to hear things said. In other cases however, the people we assume know, do not. The need to speak the unspoken to them is even more imperative.

You may say, "I tell those close to me that I love them all the time." Tell them once more. We've all heard stories of those who didn't get the chance to tell people one last time. Tell the people you love that you love them every time you see them. Make your kids almost tired of hearing you say the words.

If this essay has spoken to you, don't delay. The time to speak those unspoken words is now. Pick up the phone. Get up from your desk. Walk down the hall or to the other room. Tell them. Let them know how you feel. It may go without saying, but please don't let it go unsaid.

Fears of All Sizes

We all can deal with all kinds of fear—big and small, personal and international—better when we take action.

We can learn so much from our children.

Parker, my precious 9 year old, brought home his progress report on Friday. It showed a missing spelling assignment. We were puzzled, as we knew he had done the assignment, and asked Parker why it hadn't been turned in. He told us he had been asked to rewrite the assignment during recess. He went on to say that at the end of recess he still had one more definition to write, for the word perseverance, then he forgot to finish it and turn it in. We encouraged him to work on tasks to completion and talked about remembering to turn things in on time. We counseled him to turn it in Monday morning, that even if he wasn't going to get credit, he still needed to complete his assignment, to fulfill his commitment to his teacher.

Fast forward to Monday afternoon when we asked if he had turned in the homework. He hadn't. Fast-forward again to this morning (Tuesday), when some skillful questions from Mom helped us see the rest of the picture. Parker was intimidated to turn in the paper now. He had rewritten the words during recess, but had not finished. The main reason he didn't turn in the paper last week, or Monday morning, was not that he had forgotten, but that he was scared. Scared of being yelled at. Scared of a late assignment sheet. Scared of the great unknown.

Dad's Story

I am currently working on a very important project, and as a step in this project I want to get an audience with a pretty influential person. I built a good plan to try to get an audience with this person. If I can make this contact and persuade him to partner with me, it will go a long way towards me reaching some of my goals for this project, in fact, some of my life goals.

So I had a good plan, but I procrastinated. I didn't put the plan into effect as soon as I could have. I waited. Why? I waited because of the fear of failure, of being told "no." Will I be any further from achieving my goal if I get a "no?" Of course not. So the downside of making this contact is nil, and the upside is great. Still I procrastinated.

Fear's Definition

Parker and I both succumbed to fear. The best definition of fear I've read is found in using the word as an acronym.

F alse

E vidence

A ppearing

R eal

We both concocted situations in our heads. Situations of rejection, situations that on close examination are not likely; and even if they do occur, won't be as awful as we would think.

Father and Son

Through Parker's tears I pulled him close and hugged him. I told him I understood. I explained a bit about my current situation, mentioning that I had waited, and then once I did act, good things started to happen. (I haven't had my conversation yet, but it is looking very likely.) We talked about the best way to reduce and eliminate fear, and we determined that action is the best cure.

The World

Today is one week after the tragic attacks in the United States. There is certainly talk of fear here in the U.S. There is no doubt that there are things to be concerned about. But I am also convinced that our fears become worse when we "stew" about them—when we start thinking, "What if this?" and "What if that?" The risks in the world right now are much larger than in Parker turning in a homework assignment late. But the principles are the same.

President Bush, almost from the start, told us to "get back to work". Now a week after the tragedy, we are starting to see the wisdom in that advice. Action is a cure. Many have taken action directly related to helping, whether that is to pray, send donations, offer their time or whatever. The secret is in the action. The fear is reduced when we act. All of us have begun to get back to our lives, and that action is helping.

False Evidence Appearing Real

There are many things real in the world, but our minds have wonderful imaginations. We can build amazing scenarios to fear. Yes, our leaders need to be thinking about potentially devastating situations. Yes, there will be changes because of those possibilities. But for me as an individual, I learned my lesson from Parker this morning. We all can deal with all kinds of fear—big and small, personal and international—better when we take action.

Perseverance was the word Parker hadn't defined. In my dictionary the definition reads "the act of persevering; continued patient effort." Perseverance will help us whip our fears. Making continued patient effort will help erase the false evidence and illuminate that which is real. From our efforts and successes we will know how to deal with those real situations as they come, one at a time.

I Saw the Light

…the next time you are outside on a clear night, spend some time looking at the stars. No matter how many you can see, it will be worth your time. After all, when you've overcome all your obstacles, the stars are where you are headed.

It was a small almost insignificant event, but one I remember nearly twenty years later.

Doug, a friend of mine from college, came home to spend the weekend with me. He grew up in northwestern Indiana in the far suburbs of Chicago. I grew up on a farm in a county populated with fewer people than attended our university. One evening as we walked out in one of the fields I grew up working and playing in, Doug said, "I never knew there were so many stars!" I'd never stopped to think about it before. Growing up I'd always seen thousands of stars on a clear night. While at college I hadn't really looked at the sky much at night and hadn't paid much attention to the fact that all of the light from the buildings, cars and streetlights made it harder to see the stars. It was obvious to Doug that he could see many more stars than he had ever seen before.

We know the same number of stars are in the sky, whether

you are viewing them from Michigan or Indiana. I have thought about this brief conversation often when walking under a blanket of stars, and I've been grateful I could see so many. I also have thought of it when noticing how light it seems to be in my suburban neighborhood even in the middle of the night.

This phenomenon has a name: light pollution. Now, we have heard of all sorts of pollution but light pollution seems different. Light pollution makes sense in the world of astronomy. Scientists with very large telescopes who want to study the sky place those telescopes in uninhabited areas in part to have a very dark sky to look into. Light pollution also seems relevant if you're planning a Halloween party and want everything to be very, very dark.

However, in most situations we consider light to be a good or valuable thing—not pollution. We plan the lighting in our homes so we can see well, we plan the timing of events to make sure we will have enough light, we encourage our kids to turn the light on while reading.

Even our language shows the value we place on light. "I saw the light" (the title of this essay) is just one example of this. We do not typically think about light as being a hindrance or an obstacle in our way—which leads to my first observation.

Lessons of the Light

Read any book or listen to any speaker talk about goals, and you will learn about the importance of identifying the obstacles between us and our goals. Once we have identified the obstacles, we are to find ways to avoid or eliminate them. I agree with this approach. The story of the light sky, gives us another thing to consider, that perhaps the obstacles we face aren't always obvious.

If we aren't reaching our goals or getting the results in our lives that we want, perhaps we need to re-look at what the obstacles might be. Most obstacles are obvious and easy to see. The lesson of light pollution is that some of our obstacles are so pervasive that we don't notice them. Or, even if we do know they are there, we might not consider them to be obstacles at all!

So perhaps we don't always notice the obstacles in our way, because we can't see them.

That's where my second observation comes in. I became aware with the help of someone else. Doug's observation led me to think then and continues to make me think all these years later. We need others to help us see our world more clearly. Whether they help us identify obstacles, help us see a new part of ourselves or help us shed new light on a situation we are facing; their input is invaluable. It is in our best interest to ask for, listen to and reflect on the observations of others.

Now What?

It's time to look for the unapparent obstacles in front of you. Take some time today to open your eyes and take a fresh look at where you are. Are you achieving what you want to achieve? Are you achieving as quickly as you had hoped? What things are standing in your way?

Perhaps this questioning will lead to some obvious obstacles. If so, that's wonderful! You can then begin to work on eliminating or avoiding those obstacles. But don't stop your analysis there. Take a few more minutes to look for the pervasive things in your life—things you take for granted. You might find a new obstacle—something you previously considered to be useful that is standing in your way. It may be a person, it may be a behavior, it may be a habit. Whatever it is, once you recognize it you can begin to adjust for it.

Take time also to ask for and listen to the observations of those close to you. Consider sharing your reflections on your obstacles with someone, and then listen to the insights.

One last suggestion: the next time you are outside on a clear night, spend some time looking at the stars. No matter how many you can see, it will be worth your time. After all, when you've overcome all your obstacles, the stars are where you are headed.

It is always a good idea to watch where you are going.

Hello and Goodbye

Make the decision to be friendly, and friends will appear.

Y ou've been there. You're in a group (either by choice or by chance), and you don't know anyone. It might be professional or social—it doesn't matter, these situations can be uncomfortable.

We were two thousand miles from home stepping on a tour bus knowing almost no one. As we found a seat we noticed almost everyone already seated was a generation older than us. Since this was the first time we had ever been a part of a tour group we didn't exactly know what to expect. Internally, I thought this could be a long couple of days, trapped in planned activities on a bus with people we didn't know.

We had a tour guide, as most all tours do. She meant well and tried hard, but made a few blunders and had an interesting way of turning a phrase. Soon those phrases were leading to some soft mimicking among the group, which led to laughter, which led to people turning and getting to know each other a bit more. Don't get me wrong, this was generally a friendly group, and people had said hello and done some initial introducing at the beginning of the day, but the laughter started to really break the ice, at least for Lori and me.

As the day wore on, we started to "hang out" with two couples. Since the tour group was large, and we weren't assigned specific buses, the next morning I wondered if the whole first morning scenario would play out again. Those thoughts were quickly forgotten when our new buddies searched us out and wanted to make sure we all got on the same bus.

We spent as much time as we could with Bob and Barb and with Kurt and Beth during the rest of our trip. We ate together New Year's Eve. We led the singing of our college fight song in the restaurant. (Did I mention this tour was to the Rose Bowl?) In general it turned out that we had a great time! In fact, if I were to bet, at least one of those couples will join us on a trip to a future bowl game.

Recently, my sister was telling me of her experience during homecoming weekend at her alma mater. She and her husband met while in school, and for this, their 15th reunion, they went back and found many of their closest friends were there as well. Her children got to know the children of her friends, which led my four-year-old nephew Aaron to say, "It's really hard to make new friends, but it is even harder to say goodbye."

Making New Friends

We all have been in new situations, wondering if we would—or could—make friends. It is natural to wonder about this. Some who read this and know me may think, "Oh, come on Kevin. You are such an extrovert, this doesn't sound like something that would bother you."

Surprise.

Most of you know what I am talking about. It doesn't matter what our personality type is, building connections with new people in new situations takes some time, some risk, some luck and I believe, most importantly, some decisions.

Deciding to be Friendly

Decide to be friendly.

Making that decision means focusing on the other person.

Smile. Compliment. Say hello. Listen to their names. Use their names. All of these actions show that our focus is on them. When we start focusing on others and their needs, something magical happens: we stop worrying about ourselves and our discomfort, or insecurities, or whatever barriers we were experiencing.

Plus, our outward focus shows. People like to be noticed. They like to be called by name. They like to be smiled at. And, your friendliness helps them lose their discomfort in the situation as well. It is a very powerful truth.

Hard Work?

My nephew said it's hard to make new friends. I agree with the concept, but I'm not completely sure I agree with his word choice—but hey, he's only four!

I don't think it's *hard* to make friends per say, but it does take effort.

Make a decision to be friendly, and your apprehension will drop. Make the decision to be friendly, and friends will appear. Make the decision to be friendly, and you likely will have to say goodbye. But the time between hello and goodbye will make the effort worthwhile.

Hard work is a virtue and usually pays us big benefits. The work of making new friends, as Aaron calls it, follows this truth. It is worth the effort to make the connection. It benefits everyone. The benefits make even the difficulty of saying goodbye worth it.

Have Yourself an Awful Little Christmas

The words we use are powerful. They define our state of mind and our perspective. They help us explain the world around us.

Words are very powerful. In fact, vocabulary has a remarkably high correlation with IQ scores. We use words to communicate our thoughts and feelings. We use words to think. Having a strong vocabulary is valuable, and improving our vocabulary is a worthy self-improvement goal.

Knowing their power, I have long been fascinated by words, their origins and meanings. That fascination led me to consider a word lately. And that fascination led me to my keyboard.

But, amazingly, I'm not writing about a new, highly technical, or difficult word. I'm writing about a word that most of us use everyday. And I'm writing to tell you we all under-use or misuse it.

The Holiday Season

I find it interesting to observe behaviors and listen to conversations about the Christmas season. If you listen to shoppers they'll talk about long lines and out of stock items. They'll talk about rude clerks and over-priced merchandise. They'll talk about getting things shipped on time, finding the gift for Uncle I-Never-Know-What-To-Get-Him, eating stale fruitcakes and enduring nasty weather. They'll talk about getting presents wrapped and cookies baked and the cards mailed. They'll anguish over whether the house decorations look OK. They'll grieve over the gift they bought before it was marked down 30%.

You've heard the tirades and the stories of woe. You may have even had them or told them yourself. Somewhere in that conversation you described someone or something as "awful". Others in the conversation shook their heads in agreement.

The Christmas Season

But, during that same season, as those complaints and frustrations are voiced and heard, something else happens too. People smile more. People who rarely talk all year, whether neighbors or people whose offices are on opposite ends of the hall, stop and make a point to say "Merry Christmas." We even wish total strangers "Happy Holidays!"

We listen to an entirely different set of CDs and cassettes, and for a couple of weeks it seems the #1 song in America is "Joy to the World" or "I'll be Home for Christmas," not the latest hit from a band no one will remember in two years, People are kinder on the freeways. People are more giving and forgiving. People are more joyful. Even in the midst of the hustle and bustle, the shopping and wrapping, people still have the Christmas spirit.

When I think of these circumstances, of these positive changes in behavior, I am literally filled with awe. We seem to automatically move into the mental space of being more kind, gentle and loving, with the simple turn of the calendar.

The Word

About a week ago, I wrote down the phrase "awful vs. awe-filled" and began ruminating on that as my thesis for an essay. I was going to talk about how a couple of additional letters could change a word—and our perspective a great deal.

I decided to check my book of word origins, looking up "awful" and "awe" to see what I could learn. I learned nothing. So I went to the dictionary, and here is what I found:

Aw-ful adj. [see awe and full] 1 inspiring awe; highly impressive 2 causing fear; terrifying 3 dreadful; appalling 4 full of awe; reverential 5 very bad, ugly, unpleasant, etc. [an awful joke] *

I would bet that no one reading this uses the word awful with its number one definition. Definitions 2, 3 and 5—well, that's another story. Then I realized my dictionary is old—copyright 1988. Hmm…perhaps the meaning has changed. So I went to Dictionary.com, to get a more recent definition, and here is what I found:

> Awful adj.
> 1. Extremely bad or unpleasant; terrible: *had an awful day at the office.*
> 2. Commanding awe: "this sea, whose gently awful stirrings seem to speak of some hidden soul beneath" (Herman Melville).
> 3. Filled with awe, especially:
>   a. Filled with or displaying great reverence.
>   b. Obsolete. Afraid.
> 4. Formidable in nature or extent: *an awful burden; an awful risk.*

*definition drawn from Webster's New World Dictionary, Third College Edition, 1988

The order of the definitions is different, but the message is the same. We are shortchanging the word awful!

My earlier thesis about adding a few letters is out the window. Awful and awful; same word—two very different meanings.

While awful isn't the only word with conflicting meanings, it is a powerful example precisely because of those meanings and how different they are.

Words are powerful.

They define our state of mind and our perspective. They help us explain the world around us.

Not Just during the Holidays

I picked Christmas because while we all want to get into the spirit of the season, some seem to get there quicker and stay in that spirit longer. The people who succeed at "finding the spirit" are those who are most reverent about why we celebrate and the wonderful things that can happen during that time of year. In other words, people choosing to see the awe in the season.

While I described a whole set of positive and negative behaviors that occur during the holidays, I could do it for any celebration and any situation. I could point out what people find to be unpleasant—awful—about that time or situation and what is highly impressive—awful—about the same situation. So while I write this essay in December, the message should be clear all year. We can make a choice about which definition to use, and which definition we want to look for.

The Challenge

I see people who seem to search for things to complain about; looking for things to confirm how awful things are. We find what we look for. If I am looking for "very bad, unpleasant" things around me, I will find them. But, if I choose to look for things that "inspire awe", I will find those awful things too.

Which of those do you see during the holidays? Which do you seek the rest of the year? Recognizing that you have a choice in what you look for, which will you be looking for tomorrow?

I wish you an awful Christmas, and an awesome New Year.

Reflections of a Sports Fan

Watching people compete at something they love to do, and do exceeding well, provides me a mirror—a mirror to help me see my best self.

Many people have some affinity for sports. Sports, particularly in the United States, play a significant part in our society and consciousness. Witness the role sports had in the days and weeks after the tragedies of September 11th. Notice too that half of the top 30 rated shows in television history have been sporting events. And most recently, the Winter Olympics set records for viewers and popularity of the Games.

I'm a sports fan. I have been for as long as I can remember. I have many memories of games attended and watched. I can give you statistics and records (especially from my kidhood, when I had more time to focus on such matters). There are many sporting events I want to attend, and venues I want to see, but I already have had the privilege of attending some spectacular sporting events: the Rose Bowl, the Indianapolis 500, the Kentucky Derby, NCAA Men's basketball tournament games, and NBA Playoff games.

My son Parker is nine. From the time he was born, I have hoped he would be a sports fan. OK, first I hoped he'd be a super athlete, *then* I hoped he'd be a sports fan. Parker does not have, at this point, great athletic prowess. Parker, also, up until now, hasn't been very interested in sports. In fact, when he does watch, my wife says he does it mostly to please me.

Last Friday we were attending our nephew's high school basketball game and Parker, for the entire second half, was really into the game! He told me afterwards that, "the third and fourth quarters were awesome Dad!" As we drove home I wondered if (and hoped) there was a budding fan in the back seat ...

Why Am I a Fan?

I've often wondered why I am a sports fan. I am not a very successful athlete. My dad enjoys sports, but didn't always have a lot of discretionary time to watch sports as I grew up. But, I am a competitive person, and I've always found inspiration in watching people work hard, compete and win. That is what I get from watching sports. I read biographies of successful people for much the same reason. It is inspiring to see people reach their goals, to push themselves to new heights of achievement and success.

The meaning and value of sports has never been encapsulated so clearly to me as it was expressed in the theme for the recent Winter Olympic Games (2002)—"Light the Fire Within." Sports to me are inspiring because we can, during the best moments in sports, see the fire within the competitors and in the competition. Watching people compete at something they love to do, and do exceedingly well, provides me a mirror—a mirror to help me see my best self.

Why do I Want Parker to be a Fan?

I have probably thought more about this question than about the previous one. Do I wish for him to find the same enjoyment as I find for the 'right' reasons? Do I want him to be my sports buddy? Do I want an excuse to trade family time for sporting events? (After all, if he wants to go then it is family time, not Dad's hobby time.) Do I hope he finds positive avenues to spend some leisure time, and think participating in sports is a good choice? I believe at some point I have wanted Parker to be a sports fan for all of these reasons. But, when I really look at it, I want Parker to light his own fire within.

Perhaps Parker will find a fire for an athletic endeavor. Perhaps he will not. My hopes for him are high. If it turns out that he finds playing or watching sports to be an avocation, great. But in the end, I want him to be passionate about life and to find many ways to fuel that passion.

I don't participate in sports anymore, but the inspiration, exhilaration and learning I have gained from being a sports fan continues to fan my internal flame. My flame burns brighter as I relate my goals and achievements to athletic endeavors I have watched; whether a come-from-behind victory, a terrific team effort, a major upset, or an inspiring individual performance.

What About You?

Are you a sports fan? If not, do you know one? In either case, spend some time thinking about your connection to sports. These reflections about a passive hobby (watching sporting events rather than participating) have helped me place sports in the proper perspective in my life. Now, I am better able to decide between watching a game I "really want to see" and completing a step towards a goal. It makes it easier to turn off the game (or not even turn it on) when I could spend time with my family. It also has helped me think about my motivations as a parent.

If you are a sports fan, spend some time thinking about your motivations for being a fan. What you learn may be more powerful than a ninth inning home run, more elegant than a figure skating performance.

And if sports aren't your thing, that's OK, but recognize they can fuel passion in others in ways that are very real, even if they don't make sense to you.

Thanks!

"Who do I need to thank today?"

I t is one of the first lessons we teach our children once they
learn to talk. "Say thank you," we say. We drill it into their
minds—identifying every situation where it applies and
encouraging them to practice. In fact, I believe when my
kids were in this stage, all that practice made me better at saying
"thank you" myself. We know that saying "thank you" is not
only the socially appropriate thing to do, but it is just plain nice.
Learning to say "thank you" is an important lesson we all learn
early in life. (We also learn "please", but that is another essay
entirely.)

So why is it that as we grow up we often forget the initial,
most important, lessons? Don't get me wrong, generally most
people are pretty good at saying "thank you" when someone
does something for them.

Your neighbor brings you a loaf of bread. You naturally say
"thanks." A co-worker helps you when you are in a time crunch,
and you thank them for their time and effort. These are the
types of situations we are teaching our children to recognize and
to share gratitude for.

There are other situations however where we all can do
much better at offering "thanks."

The Dress

This one occurs every day in hallways and offices and other places where people meet. Someone notices how nicely a woman is dressed and compliments her, "Nice dress!" Then—without thinking—she shifts her eyes downward, looks at her dress, maybe even pointing at it, and replies, "This old thing? I've had it forever."

What has the dress wearer just done? Well, she has just publicly announced that the person who complimented her has bad judgment. I know, that isn't necessarily what the she was trying to do, but in reality that's exactly what's happening. When we don't accept compliments or verbally shrug them off, we are in effect saying we don't agree, and that he or she has poor taste or judgment. Maybe it isn't your favorite dress. Maybe you think you look better in red. Maybe you *have* had it for years. In any case, someone thinks you look nice, and took the effort to say so. Take a lesson from our children. Whether you agree or not, simply say "thank you."

The Shot

Women aren't the only ones who fall prey to this mistake. Men, ever been on the golf course and had someone tell you, you just made a good shot? Maybe you like to fish and someone complimented you on your latest catch. How many times in these situations have you heard someone say (or said yourself) "It was just luck," or "I'll never be able to make that shot again," or "I wish it had been a little further left?" Next time replace this commentary with a simple "thank you.".

The Breakfast of Champions

We know that generally we are comfortable in thanking people when something is *done* for us because that's what we've been taught. It's socially acceptable, and pretty much expected.

It is equally important to provide a gracious comment when people have given us feedback. Why? Because people will be more willing to give us feedback repeatedly if we show our appreciation. Since feedback, which has been called "the breakfast of champions," is useful for our growth and understanding we want to keep getting it. If we don't psychologically reward people for giving us the feedback, that feedback will dry up and go away. At the same time, when we share our gratitude for the feedback, we improve our chance of receiving more—and— more importantly, we improve the self-image of the other person. A simple thank you in these situations is truly a win-win response.

The Written Thank You

With the advent of the email, cell phones, pagers, and other forms of instant communication, I hear and read of the decline of letter writing. All of these tools are great. (Please continue to share your gratitude using these modern tools!) But, none of these great tools provides as powerful or lasting impact as does a simple, handwritten, thank you note.

As you practice acknowledging your gratitude, don't forget the handwritten notes. I am amazed how few people take the time to write and send them. I have some that were sent to me years ago that I *never* plan to throw away. I would guess you can say the same thing.

I make a conscious effort to be thankful in writing. In fact, it is on my ongoing to-do list as "Who do I need to thank today?". This conscious decision has helped me grow more gracious in my overall attitude and spirit. At the same time, it helps strengthen my relationships with others.

Your Attitude of Gratitude

How can you strengthen and deepen your own attitude of gratitude?

Right now, resolve to be more gracious with others, remembering to simply say "thank you" when someone pays you a compliment.

Right now, think of two people to whom you could write a thank you, whether the act was yesterday or six years ago. Write those notes today.

Lastly, find places and situations to thank people when they might not expect it. For example, I always thank flight attendants and pilots as I leave an airplane. By giving them solid eye contact and saying "thank you," I am strengthening my graciousness making them smile and putting a bounce in my step as I leave the plane. Again, everybody wins.

A simple lesson learned as children is more powerful than we may have ever realized. Make the time today to become more grateful—just say "thanks."

Thanks for reading.

Pretty Please (With Sugar on Top)

When we say "please" in a spirit of gratefulness and with the willingness to offer help in return, then we are not only being polite and pragmatic, but authentic and genuine. We are communicating with another person with our heart rather than our head.

My daughter Kelsey isn't quite four. She is a wonderful girl, and I love her dearly. She is, however, sometimes a little bossy. With a demanding tone, she will declare what will happen next. With emphasis, she will tell me what to do. These aren't behaviors her mother and I want to become habits. Not to mention that they just don't sit very well with me!

Thankfully, others have told us that when she is with them, she is very polite and well mannered. A welcome relief, yes, but it doesn't reduce our angst about her bossy behavior. Last week, as a way to positively reinforce the behaviors we are looking for, I tried something new.

Word of the Week

Last week, I declared that "please" was the "Word of the Week." My intent was to remind all of us in the house of the importance of asking rather than demanding. I vowed to both Parker and Kelsey that I would be reminding them of the word, that they would be praised for using it, and that I was going to work on using it more as well.

I was proud of my idea, and the approach did raise awareness (somewhat), but you'll never guess what the "Word of the Week" is this week. Yep, it is still please! We are making progress, but we aren't there yet—the 39-year-old and 3-year-old alike.

An Early Lesson

Saying "please" and "thank you" are two of the first phrases we teach children. We do this because they are important phrases that represent basic values. I recently wrote an essay about "thank you," and now I find myself focusing on "please." Maybe I'm a slow learner since I'm still trying to master these childhood lessons.

I can remember when Parker was little, taking him to visit his great grandparents for the first time after he could talk. One of the last things I told him before we went inside was, "Remember to say please." In some odd way, Parker saying "please" was supposed to prove I was doing my job as a parent. Maybe you haven't felt that feeling, but I am sure you have seen praise lavished on little ones when they've said "please." "Please" is definitely an early lesson engrained in all of us.

The Importance of Asking

"Ask and it shall be given to you; seek and you will find; knock and the door will be opened to you. For everyone who asks receives;

he who seeks finds; he who knocks, the door will be opened."
—*Matthew 7:7–8, NIV*

You have to ask if you want to receive. Without asking, you cannot get. This profound truth can be stated in a variety of ways, but the different words don't change the message. Being willing to ask is important to our development, to our comfort, and to our success—reaching our goals, both large and small.

When we are teaching children about saying "please" it is in the context of asking for something. We don't just say please, we add the word to some sort of request. We tell them that saying please is the nice, or proper, thing to do. We really are trying to teach them that it is more polite, more socially acceptable, to say "please" than to simply demand that their wish is granted.

Adding the Sugar

Asking with a "please" makes any request a bit easier to receive. It's like putting a little sugar with the request. We learn that the verbal sugar of "please" can help us, just like Mary Poppins taught us —"A spoonful of sugar helps the medicine go down, in the most delightful way."

Maybe that is why when we are little and we REALLY want something, we embellish "please" to something like the title of this essay.

So we are teaching children that "please" is not only the nice thing to do, but also that it will probably help us get what we ask for. (Have you ever withheld something from a child until they said the "magic word?")

But is there more to it than that?

More than a Word

Yes, I am trying to teach my children to use the word, but beyond the vocabulary lesson, I want them to learn the attitude of graciousness. Saying "please" is both polite and pragmatic—and important for both reasons. But it goes beyond being polite. It goes beyond being pragmatic.

When we say "please" in a spirit of gratefulness and with the willingness to offer help in return, then we are not only being polite and pragmatic, but authentic and genuine. We are communicating with another person with our heart rather than our head.

Final Thoughts

The practice and attitude of saying "please" is a powerful one. That is why we teach it so early. Think about your habits and attitudes around this important phrase. Ask yourself the following questions.

- How consistently do I use "please?"
- How often do I type it in an email or letter?
- How consistently do I include "please" in requests to those closest to me?

Take the time to think about these things today.

Please?

Thank you.

Passages

Age, like beauty, is in the eye of the beholder. I believe one of the keys to a full, vital life is learning.

Today, as I write this, my mother turns sixty. Less than two weeks ago, my oldest son turned ten. A week before that, I celebrated my 40th birthday. And just a couple of days before that, we proudly watched our nephew graduate as valedictorian of his high school class.

With such a confluence of big days coming in such a short time, I have been thinking about time, age and stages of life. And, as is often the case, when I start thinking, eventually, I start writing.

Evan

Evan's graduation came first. Every graduation is significant. But, when the graduate you are going to see addresses his class, it is extra special. Throughout the evening, I reflected on my high school graduation, and I could remember the feelings and thoughts I had as I graduated (even though it was many years ago). I could see those kids feeling and thinking many of the same things.

Evan told his classmates that they were being given a ticket to "the Big Show…the greatest adventure of their lives." He went on to talk about success and shared his philosophy (how many eighteen-year-olds have a philosophy?).

"I believe success is not something you hold, but something you feel. It is not about material possessions, it is about self-ful-fillment. Remember the first time you wrote your name in cursive letters or tied your shoes all by yourself? Remember the day you passed your driving test or felt the excitement of winning a big game? Success at these moments is not about owning something; it is about knowing and extending yourself."

Wise words from an eighteen year old; words we can all reflect on and learn from.

Kevin

I experienced an odd mix of personal emotions during Evan's ceremony. On one hand, I am clearly grown up—just check my driver's license and increasingly gray hair. On the other hand, I didn't feel all that different from the Austin High graduates. I too feel at a point of commencement. My work on several projects seems close to coming to fruition, which will lead me to a new stage of my life, and will give me a new ticket. At the same time, these new opportunities will necessarily change some of my past priorities and work. These are exciting and new times, just like a graduate.

This essay is in part about age, but I've never really gotten very hung up about age. I've generally felt age is just a number. One of the best gifts I received for my birthday were the words written on more than one card that said I was the youngest forty year old they knew! Even so, forty is sort of a milestone, and while I haven't been sad about it, I have been a bit introspective. It isn't a crisis, but it is a commencement.

Parker

Parker is in double digits. My son is ten!

We often think of thirteen as the start of the teenage years, but ten seems monumental to me. Things are already changing. Parker and I are starting to be interested in some of the same books. As a matter of fact, I am reading a book now that belongs to him. (I hope that happens many times in my life.)

He is starting to enjoy movies with more complex stories and themes. His mind is strong and sharp, and he is really growing up. His tastes in activities are changing. All of these changes are wonderful gifts not only to him, but also to me, as I am being given new opportunities to learn and grow both as a parent and a person.

Mom

I was blessed with young parents. While I can't imagine having a twenty-year-old now (which I was when Mom turned forty), I love that in some ways my sister and I grew up with our parents. And now, since she and my father are in good health, I love that we can experience many things together as adults. I look forward to doing that for many more years.

Mom has a full head of silver hair, and has had for many years. This fact belies her mental youth. She is active, curious and young at heart. She has many hobbies and interests and is continuously learning.

Age, like beauty, is in the eye of the beholder. I believe one of the keys to a full, vital life is learning. As it turns out, learning is a common thread through Evan, Parker, Mom and me. As each of us pass through a milestone, learning is playing a key role in "extending ourselves" in our life success.

I've used these recent events as an opportunity to reflect on stages of life and what I can learn from them. You may be far from a milestone, but we all can benefit from reflecting on our stage in life—whatever it may be. Take that time. You won't regret the investment in yourself.

Slug Bug Black, No Tag Backs

As humans we get to choose what to look for. Optimists look for the silver lining, and see it. Pessimists look for the rain, and find it. We get to choose.

The first time I ever heard this phrase was last winter when my son suddenly slapped me—while I was driving—and said, "Slug bug silver no tag backs." I was SO confused. What did he just say, why did he say it, and why did he hit me!

I soon learned that this is a car game (you know, a game you play to pass the time in the car). When you see a Volkswagen Beetle (the "slug bug"), you say "slug bug *insert the appropriate color here*," and hit (or hopefully just tap) the other person.

I thought the game seemed very strange and asked Parker where he learned to play. He said, "Everyone knows that game Dad" (with the implied "duh" in his voice). I turned to my wife, and she knew the game too. Apparently I was the only one in the dark!

I grew up playing lots of car games, but this one never

made it to our car. Since that initial introduction, Slug Bug has become an on-again/off-again event in our car...see a Beetle and utter the catchy phrase (we've mostly eliminated the "slugging" part).

The Long Drive

Last week Parker and I set off on a long car drive together. We decided to make this an ongoing game during our trip and keep track of how many times we "tagged" each other throughout the trip. I am happy to say that I won. (OK, so I'm a little competitive.) But in Parker's defense, I will say it was easier for me to win since he was reading or playing his Game Boy some of the time as I drove. It is hard to see the "slug bugs" when you're not even looking out of the car!

We got creative, tagging for billboards and other pictures of Beetles. It was a fun game. And at some point, as I watched the other side of the Interstate for "slug bugs," I got the message.

They are *everywhere*!

Not Just Beetles

A few years ago we bought a new car. We loved our new black Ford Expedition. Right after we bought it, I began to see Expeditions everywhere! On ads, in parking lots, on the streets—they were everywhere. It was amazing! It was as if everyone had decided to buy an Expedition at the same time we did.

Of course, that's not true. There were Expeditions on the road before we bought ours, but I didn't notice them. What was different? I noticed them now because I was paying attention. In the past, I didn't care so my mind just filtered them out. I've shared this story with others, and they have had a similar experience; perhaps you have too.

Then it was Expeditions, now it is Beetles. I'm looking for

them, and I'm seeing them.

The Reticular Activating System

The technical reason this occurs is due to a part of our brain called the reticular activating system (RAS). The RAS is like a filtering system for the brain. It helps us sort what we see, and it brings to our consciousness those things that we tell ourselves are important.

This is why two people can go to a movie and have entirely different experiences. One person feels the power was in the relationship in the story; the other is touched by the cinematography. If you've ever experienced that—or had very different responses to the same movie after watching it a second or third time—you can thank your RAS.

The reticular activating system helps us explain assumptions, and prejudices, and lots more in our lives. RAS is what keeps us from being in constant sensory overload. All of those ideas (assumptions, prejudices and more) could warrant an essay, but let me share what I learned while watching for slug bugs.

We See What We Are Looking For

That's it.

That's the whole message.

We see what we are looking for—that is the job of our reticular activating system. Amazingly, it comes as a part of our human package. What a great thing! Even better though is how you can use this capability. As humans we get to choose what we look for. Optimists look for the silver lining, and see it. Pessimists look for the rain, and find it. We get to choose.

If you are looking for opportunities, you will find them. If you have goals set, the answers to your obstacles will be found. We see what we are looking for.

Last week, I was looking for slug bugs, and thanks to that simple game, now I am looking for a whole lot of new things in my life. What are you looking for? Is it a conscious choice?

Think about those questions today. And think about them the next time you see a Beetle—it probably will be sooner than you think.

Slug bug black, no tag backs!

The Good Stuff

*So often in our busy lives we forget what really matters; the
things that make us smile and cry. The things we'll remember
forever or miss when they are gone.*

L ast night, at the Indiana State Fair, Lori and I saw
Kenny Chesney in concert. If you don't know, he is a
country singer who has had enough hits for a greatest
hits album. (Am I showing my age by calling it an
album?) Because of my farm background and antique tractor
hobby, I am partial to his hit *She Thinks My Tractor's Sexy*, but
last night the lyrics to his latest single really struck me.

The song talks about a young man having his first fight
with his wife, and—after driving around for a while—he ends
up in a bar. He tells the bartender he wants the good stuff, but
the bartender tells him that he can't find that in the bar.

The bartender goes on to describe "the good stuff." Here is
one portion:

"Cause it's the first long kiss on a second date.

Momma's all worried when you get home late.

And droppin' the ring in the spaghetti plate,

Cause your hands are shakin' so much.

And it's the way that she looks with the rice in her hair.
Eatin' burnt suppers the whole first year
And asking for seconds to keep her from tearin' up.
Yeah, man, that's the good stuff."

The Song and Me

OK, I didn't drop Lori's ring on any plate, and she has rarely burnt a meal. But the phrase, though I had heard the song before, really hit me. "The Good Stuff."

So often in our busy lives we forget what really matters; the things that make us smile and cry. The things we'll remember forever or miss when they are gone. So with apologies to the songwriters and to Mr. Chesney, I thought I would share with you some of my "good stuff."

Here's a short list just from yesterday…

- State Fair food.
- Driving one of my tractors in a tractor parade.
- A hard rain after a long dry spell.
- Sitting next to my wife at a concert we could enjoy together.
- Saluting the flag during the Star Spangled Banner.

And then a more general list…

- Watching a sunset on Lake Michigan.
- My son's laugh.
- Eating homemade ice cream.
- Listening to my Grandpa tell me stories about when he farmed.
- Singing *Hail Purdue* at a sporting event.

- Walking hand in hand with Lori.
- Spending time with old friends.
- Playing a game of Scrabble with my Mom.
- Sledding down a snow-covered hill.
- A hug from my daughter.
- Riding on a dirt road with my Dad looking at fields of crops.
- Smelling lilacs in the spring.
- Sitting in front of a roaring fire in my fireplace.
- Watching the *Sound of Music* again.

I could have written a really long list, but you get the idea. Just like with the song, my stuff may not be your stuff.

What's Your Good Stuff?

I received a blessing by thinking about those important touchstone experiences. As you can see both from the song and my list, they aren't necessarily big things. And while we may share some common things on our lists, in general, everyone's "good stuff" will be distinct and unique.

Take the time to think about those important, significant things in your life. Take the time to think about your own "good stuff."

Your list may not become a hit song, but it will be a blessing.

Notes:

Special thanks to Craig Wiseman and Jim Collins who wrote the song, *The Good Stuff.*

If you want to read all of the song's lyrics, go to: http://www.lyricsondemand.com/k/kennychesneylyrics/the-goodstufflyrics.html

U-Pick

When we focus only on the exterior or superficial, we miss the depth of others. It is only in that depth that we will truly know them, and ultimately, appreciate them.

My mother emailed me about an experience she had last week that reminded me of some of my experiences growing up, and I hope you can relate as well. I'll let her tell you the first part of the story…

"It was a beautiful, early September day in Michigan. The temperature was balmy with a nice breeze. It is days like these that remind me why I love living here so much. My husband, John, and I drove to a 'u-pick' blueberry patch a short distance from our home. We were told to pick from any bush, and we quickly noticed that the berries were plentiful. It didn't take long however to notice something very interesting. There were plenty of berries on the outsides of the bushes, but if you looked inside, the berries were bigger, even more bountiful and virtually untouched."

After telling me this story, Mom went on to say, "It occurred to me that it is the same with our relationships. How many times do we just look on the outside or on the surface and not really work at our relationships to know the inner self of others?"

Mom is right (of course moms always are, aren't they?).

It is a powerful lesson. We fall in love with the berries on the exterior, but when we look inside we find even better berries. So it is in our lives. When we focus only on the exterior or superficial we miss the depth of others. It is only in that depth that we will truly know them and, ultimately, appreciate them.

If Mom had followed the lead of the other pickers and hadn't looked to the interior, she would have been disappointed by her harvest—and wouldn't have had as many berries to enjoy. Regardless of how many berries could be found outside, Mom and John picked the whole bush.

My mother (in reference to a running joke about her height) mentioned that she had to pick inside the bush because she couldn't reach all of them on the outsides of the bushes. I know better. I know she picked inside for two reasons: she knew from experience there would be good berries there, and she is a good gardener and knows all the fruit needs to be harvested to help the plant thrive.

It reminds me that when we have experience at something, it is important to use it! Mom knew picking the whole bush, inside and out, would help the plant thrive—and she trusted her instincts (used her experience) regardless of what the other pickers were doing. We know when we get to know people at deeper levels they thrive—and so do we. We all need attention and care and love, and without the proper care and environment, just like the blueberry bush, we won't thrive.

Just like the blueberry patch, our lives are "U-Pick". You decide what kind of relationships you want to build. You decide how deep you want to look when trying to understand and relate to others. When we pick the right patches, we will find lots of great fruit, but the sweetest fruit will always be found when we look a little deeper. It takes a bit more effort and time, but you will be well rewarded.

Think about the lessons of the blueberry patch the next time you are building a relationship, whether with your long, lost cousin, a new neighbor, or the new colleague down the hall. "U-Pick" your approach—just remember, your choice will determine the relationship you harvest.

Go Tell It on The Mountain

Be grateful for the gift of the experience. If this is an experience you shared with others, thank them for helping make it so wonderful for you.

W hen I was 16 I attended a youth conference in Estes Park, Colorado. The whole week was wonderful, but a couple particular events were really special. I (and the small group I was with) called these events "mountain-top" experiences.

I remember other "mountain-top" experiences at Lake Tahoe with Lori where we had quiet afternoons in the sun on large rocks at lake level. But last week, I believe, I took personal mountain-top experiences to new "heights."

My family and I were in Hawaii on the island of Maui. Early in our week we drove to the top of Haleakala, an inactive volcano on the island. We left early in the morning, but we didn't get to the summit in time to experience sunrise. We had a great time on the mountain—climbing, exploring and taking pictures. We resolved to come back later in the week, making sure we were there in time for the sunrise. (You know it's cool when your four- and ten-year-olds *want* to get up extra early to make it in time for sunrise!)

We determined to make our return trip on Thursday. We left our condo about 5 a.m. (45 minutes earlier than our first trip), and as we drove along the ocean we were captivated by the brilliant full moon—so captivated that we stopped to take pictures as its light shone across the still waters of the Pacific. About two-thirds of the way up the volcano, the National Park Ranger told us we would have to hurry to make sunrise. As we finished our drive, Lori and I planned a strategy. I suggested that I take the video,and she take pictures. (She is the much better photographer, so this was an easy call.) We planned so we could get pictures quickly if needed.

Throughout the winding (*very* winding) climb we continued to comment on the full moon. Even as the sky was slowly transforming from night into a morning sky, the moon maintained its luster. As we reached the top I was thinking that the moon alone was worth the trip—wondering if the sunrise could possibly be any better.

We arrived in the parking lot, and saw many people poised with cameras. It was clear we weren't too late! As Lori prepared to take pictures, Parker said he wanted to climb White Hill. This short but steep hike is one we had taken on our earlier trip. I knew he liked the view from there—I did too. I started to follow him, but I didn't want to miss the sunrise on the walk. Parker was well on his way, and Lori needed solitude to take pictures, so Kelsey and I started walking up White Hill.

I wanted to film, needed to watch my step, and had to help Kelsey and hold her hand. We made good progress, and moved up the hill to a point were I could see back to the east. On the horizon I knew the sun would rise soon. So I urged Kelsey to stand beside me and watch the sun. I turned on the camera and started by looking the other way at that amazing full moon;

then turned to catch the entire sunrise on video.

Seldom in my life have I been so awed.

Parker witnessed the sunrise from the top of White Hill, Kelsey and I part way up, and Lori from a couple hundred feet below.

A few minutes later we were together again at the top of White Hill. For a few moments I was overcome with emotion. I had just experienced indescribable beauty, and had the good fortune to share it with the people I love the most. I paused, reflected, took a deep breath and immediately added these moments to my list of "mountaintop" experiences.

As the day wore on and we frolicked in the ocean, I thought about the morning. There are only 12, sometimes 13, full moons each year. Certainly, the sky would be cloudy for some of them, so the chance of having the experience we had has to be rare. And since we don't live on Maui, for me it was likely a once in a lifetime moment.

Off the Mountain

Certainly not all of my most magical, memorable and meaningful experiences have taken place at altitude. Regardless, I still call them "mountain-top experiences." You might call them by different names, but you've had these experiences just the same. My most recent high got me thinking about these experiences.

There are four things we can do to enrich our lives even further by these types of moments (whatever you choose to call them): be aware, recognize them, remember them and be grateful.

Be Aware

The first step to blessing your life with these experiences is to be aware of their existence! Recognize that they can show up in the seemingly most mundane and ordinary situations and locations. Being aware, almost expectant, will help you catch more of them.

Recognize Them

You have to notice them—as they are occurring! On Haleakala, I recognized what was an amazing set of circumstances, all leading to a wonderful moment. When we can recognize these experiences—in the moment—our appreciation of them is heightened.

Remember Them

This is easier if you have done the last step of recognizing them. When we recognize the wonder of the moment—as it is occurring, we can do some simple things to help remember it better.

Take a moment, in the moment, to take it all in. Close your eyes; remember the sounds and the smells. Open your eyes and take mental pictures that you can refer to anytime you want to remember the situation. Consciously engaging your senses with your brain in a "let's remember this" challenge will help you more easily return to the magical time and place.

If you are a writer or keep a journal, writing about the experience later is another way to keep the details real and the memory stronger.

Be Grateful

Be grateful for the gift of the experience. If this is an experience you shared with others, thank them for helping make it so wonderful for you. Based on my beliefs, I thanked God for creating the Hawaii moment. I encourage you to express your gratitude in ways consistent with your beliefs. A deep sense of gratitude for the experience will deepen and enrich it even further.

Final Thoughts

I'm down from the mountain now. I know that my description of what we experienced cannot do it justice, and for that I apologize. On the other hand, my main goal is to get you thinking about your own mountain-top moments.

It doesn't matter if you haven't thought about this before, or if you have but haven't followed my "formula." Take some time soon to reflect over the moments you would call most magical. Remember them and be grateful for them now.

And begin living in an awareness and expectancy that you'll add a new one soon. Who knows, maybe it will be today.

Note—The picture of me on the cover was taken just minutes after the sun came up that morning.

And the Wall Came Tumbling Down

*For us it is often true that the biggest challenge ends up
being a blessing to us in the end, even while we might
be cursing it at the time!*

Last week, I helped my Dad put a hole in a wall of the
house where I grew up. Dad is remodeling the house
and needed a new entry from the partial basement into
the crawl space. This is not a new home. We don't know
for sure, but it is safe to say that the wall we were going to work
on is at least 100 years old.

The Task

Dad had been thinking about how to do this job for some
time and decided to rent a machine that cuts concrete, using a
diamond tipped blade. He felt that with that machine, and
some work with a sledgehammer, in a couple of hours we could
complete the task. So, on my visit, we rented the saw and began
the job.

The saw is designed to cut up to about four inches deep.
The wall is more like seven inches thick. The saw is heavy and

probably would work marvelously on a floor. We were using it to cut into a wall, above our heads. The saw works great on concrete, but not so well on rock. We quickly learned that the wall had some large rocks in it—it wasn't just concrete as it appears from the surface.

All in all, I hope this description is letting you see that after a couple of minutes, we realized this was going to be a much tougher job than we had hoped or imagined.

The Modifications

After some initial cuts with the saw, and some pounding with a sledge hammer, we went for some more tools. Specifically, we picked up a small hammer and a chisel. We took turns using the saw, using the sledgehammer, and then chipping away at the concrete around the now-revealed large stones with the small hammer and chisel.

We developed a strategy—switch the tools based on what you saw. Stay focused on one part of the wall at a time. All the while reminding ourselves that, once we broke through, our job would be easier.

The Completion

Our observations were right. Once we got a small breakthrough, the hole was quickly completed. In fact, the part of the wall that had been our biggest obstacle, the large and very hard stones, became our ally. Once one of those was out, the concrete around them moved easily, which loosed the next large stone, until the hole was complete.

The Lessons

I thought about our task as I drove home from my Dad's— the process *and* the lessons that were revealed. I learned about much more than just about breaking through concrete. I learned some keys to overcoming any obstacles in our lives—about breaking through the walls between where we are and our goals.

Have a plan. Dad had thought about the project and had a plan for completing the job. We all need to have plans for achieving our goals—including breaking through the walls.

Have help. Part of Dad's plan was to have someone else there. The saw was heavy, and it was important that someone else was around. Having two people allowed us to spell each other, and make all the effort at the wall come with full strength. It is just as true with our goals. We will be more successful, more quickly, when we collaborate and are willing to ask for help, guidance and support.

Have a wide array of tools. Each of the tools we ended up using was helpful. The small hammer could reach places in a more targeted way than the sledge. The chisel helped us focus even more than the saw. The saw, while it wasn't as helpful as we had hoped, did provide a valuable part of the solution. We need to collect a wide tool kit to help us get through our obstacles as well—the bigger our kits of ideas and skills and experiences, the more successful we will be.

The obstacle can be tougher than we think. Once we saw how hard the saw was to handle, and once we saw the big rocks, we realized the job might be tougher than we originally thought. When we face an obstacle, we sometimes think it will come down easily. When it doesn't, we can get discouraged. Just remember, that the discouragement is a temporary inconvenience. Get past it and keep working.

The wall seemed immovable. Do your obstacles ever feel immovable? Have you noticed that sometimes you keep working and working on something and never seem to make any progress? There were many swings of the sledgehammer that didn't seem to do a thing. It took a lot of effort for very little—

apparent—progress at the start. In the end though, it is easy to see that every blow against the wall played a part in our success. The same is true for our other walls.

The big rocks made it harder. The big rocks were hard! The saw didn't cut them well; they didn't give or move with a swing of the sledge; and the chisel was useless against them. We all will encounter the big rocks in our walls. That's life. Move on. We worked on the softer concrete around them, rather than focusing on them directly. We often can do the same thing as we move through whatever obstacles we face.

The big rocks made it easier. Paradoxically, in the end, the big rocks actually made our job easier. Why? Because once we had one of them out, other pieces, including other big rocks, came out easier than if it had been a wall of "just concrete." For us it is often true that the biggest challenge ends up being a blessing to us in the end, even while we might be cursing it at the time! (I won't comment on whether there was any cursing in the basement that day).

Once you have a small breakthrough you are almost there! Lots of effort for little progress, then with a relatively small breakthrough, you are almost done. I've read that something like 90% of the energy used by the space shuttle for its entire mission is used in the first few seconds after liftoff. Invest the effort up front, and when the wall *starts* to come down, get ready, you're almost there!

Maybe you've never swung a hammer to bust a piece of concrete. It doesn't matter because I know you have faced at least one obstacle between you and your goals. I am also sure you will face another. I hope the lessons I learned can be valuable to you the next time you are staring at your concrete wall.

I'll Take Mine
Hand Cranked

One of the wonders of our children is their ability to live in the moment. Eating homemade ice cream is one of those times where we must do the same—it won't be as magically good tomorrow as it is right now.

Sitting at lunch after a Saturday meeting, and the topic of homemade ice cream comes up. Recipes are discussed and I mention the new White Mountain freezer I got for Christmas. (In case you're wondering—6 quart, just like the one we had growing up.) Somewhere in the conversation I assert that ice cream is definitely better if it is hand cranked; the only way to make ice cream with my new freezer.

Then my friend Bob Ferling suggests I write a *Vantagepoints* about this topic, and I think (and probably say) something like, "I don't think I could write an entire piece on homemade ice cream."

Now, two days later, with a clearer head (and the memory of homemade ice cream from last night in my mind—and on my tongue), it's clear I *can* write about homemade ice cream—and what making and eating it can teach us.

The Recipe

I stumbled onto my recipe. It's not the one my Mom or Grandmother used, and with all due respect to both of them, I like mine better. The ice cream can only be as good as the recipe and its ingredients allow. This is true for all things in life. What you sow, you reap. Following the success principles of others will more likely lead you to similar success. If you use better ingredients, you'll get better ice cream.

Hand Cranking

I know that sometime in my kidhood I heard people say the ice cream is better if it's hand cranked. I also recall side, sly remarks made between "hand crankers" when people mentioned they had an electric ice cream maker implying these people were impostors. Whether the ice cream is *really* any different is highly debatable. But what is important, to me at least, is the cranking itself.

Cranking ice cream requires knowledge—knowing how much salt to put with your ice, how much water to add to the mixture, and how to layer these ingredients; skill—cranking at just the right rate makes for better ice cream; and planning and patience—it takes time to do it well, you can't make ice cream in five minutes.

Hand cranking, in my experience, is something you do after dinner, so everyone has time to "make some room for desert." It also gives people (often "the men") some time to chat and connect while the mixture is magically transforming to ice cream. We need to take the time for fellowship and conversation. Hand cranking makes us slow down—not a bad thing in our fast paced lives.

The Enjoyment

Few foods rival really good homemade ice cream. The special thing about it is not just that it's good, but since it doesn't store very well, it's a treat for right now. Homemade ice cream is best enjoyed immediately, in the moment. One of the wonders of our children is their ability to live in the moment. Eating homemade ice cream is one of those times where we must do the same—it won't be as magically good tomorrow as it is right now. Homemade ice cream reminds me how sweet life can be when we live in the now.

The Tradition

Homemade ice cream is a part of my growing up, and it holds a special place in my mind—and in my palate.

I consider myself forward-looking, flexible and willing to change—more so than many people. But there are some things that are better left unchanged. The challenge is determining which things not to change and understanding why.

I don't care what others may say, I think its better hand cranked.

The Words Do Matter

Words can make a big difference in the lives of others, and in our lives as well. The words do matter.

Air Canada Flight 154

I was boarding a flight in Edmonton, Alberta, bound for Toronto after a long day. As I handed my boarding pass to the Air Canada gate agent, I asked her if she was having a good day. Her response has been in my mind for nearly two weeks. She looked at me, smiled, and said, "All the better for you asking me, thanks."

As I literally skipped down the jet way, I smiled. I have asked hundreds of people if they are having a good day. Never have I received that response. I've heard, "Its OK," "No, not really," and "Fine, thanks." But never, until now, have I heard, "All the better for you asking me, thanks."

Her response was gracious and warm. It wowed me as a customer—giving me a very positive experience with Air Canada—even before I was on the plane! More importantly, it made me feel special as a human being. Maybe she was taught to say this by a parent at a young age and it simply was an automatic response. Even if this were true, her genuine response makes that irrelevant.

What would have been a normal flight was changed by eight words—eight words I am sure I will never forget.

The Internet Essay

Recently I read an essay from one of my favorite writers. Scott Ringwelski writes an essay each week called Positive Pause. Last week's issue starts:

> "No Problem'…actually is.
>
> 'No problem.' It seems natural, easy going, off the cuff, casual.
>
> It's a throwaway line for a disposable world.
>
> However, how does your throwaway line and casual attitude translate to those you say it to?"

Scott goes on to say that the two words are actually two negatives, no and problem. Through a wonderful personal story he relates that rather than answering a request with "no problem," it would be much more meaningful and powerful to say "It would be my pleasure." Scott knows, as does my Edmonton friend, that choosing these words can make a huge difference.

Rhea

A few hours ago my stepmother passed away. While there are many ways she blessed my life, and there will be many things I will remember about her, the thing that strikes me now is one of her favorite phrases. "Terrific!"

Ask Rhea how she was, and she, more often than not, would say "Terrific!" Even over the last few months when she was very ill. When you saw her, or spoke to her on the phone, if you asked how she was, she would say, "Terrific!"

Certainly in these last few months she hasn't always been terrific, at least by most people's standards. Her optimistic reply though, always lifted my day—even if I were calling to try and lift hers.

The Common Thread

In all these cases, the words chosen by people have made a positive impact on those around them. As a consultant if I think about these word choices, I could easily make a case that using these phrases would be powerful in terms of customer service, and internal communications.

Most importantly though is that choosing these words transforms the people who say them. Think about my Air Canada friend saying, "All the better for you asking me, thanks!", or anyone saying "It's been a pleasure," or "Terrific!"

These phrases recast our thinking and our self-talk in a more positive, focused and accountable way. Indeed, these words can make a big difference in the lives of others, and in our lives as well.

The words do matter. To everyone.

It's Our Choice

Choosing frustration can lead to regret, anger, resentment and more. Choosing fascination can lead to understanding, knowledge, and improved results and relationships (and more).

S o much of our perspective and how we respond to the world around us relates to what we choose to think about. Recently I heard a phrase that is drastically changing my response to many situations. Over time, as this becomes my habit, it is going to help me with some behaviors I've wanted to change for a long time.

I was listening to a Jim Rohn CD as I drove to a meeting. Jim said, "Why not choose fascination rather than frustration?" He went on to say that he used to get frustrated much more often than he does now. Why? In part because, now, rather than choosing to be frustrated by a situation, he chooses to be fascinated instead. He went on to say he still gets frustrated sometimes, but this mental shift had made a positive impact on his life.

I am a very positive person, but I do get frustrated. I get frustrated when my computer won't do what I want it to do. I get frustrated by my children's behavior when, at times, it doesn't match my expectations. Many days I get frustrated by my own inability to get as much done as I would like. I could go on, but that list wouldn't make for very good reading.

Sometimes I Get It

Upon reflecting on Jim's observation I realized I already am pretty good at this, in some parts of my life. When the source of the frustration is outside of my control—an airport delay or traffic tie-up are two that immediately come to my mind—I have been able to reduce my own frustration.

In fact, I have often found it enjoyable and enlightening to focus on the hilarity of other peoples' responses to these situations. I can think of more than one time while in a car, or a line of some sort, when I was smiling and chuckling inside at the clearly counterproductive behaviors of those around me. Without realizing it, I was moving to an observer perspective, which was leading me to be more fascinated and less frustrated.

With My Computer

A functioning computer is one of the most important business assets I possess. Over the past few months I have had some nagging problems with my laptop—all related to the fact that I needed more memory and a bigger hard drive. It clearly was time for a new machine. When I first started encountering some intermittent problems, I would throw my own little pity party—and be frustrated while trying to solve the problem. The problem with a pity party is that while you are partying, you aren't focused on moving forward. I like going to parties—and am seldom the first to leave—but this isn't the kind of party where it pays to linger.

Eventually I realized the partying had to stop. As I began to notice the signs of impending problems, I was able to reduce the severity of those problems. As I paid attention (became fascinated), I learned how to recover from these problems more quickly.

I write this on my new laptop; and the problems of the last one are quickly fading into mere memories. The lesson hasn't though—with the new machine comes new versions of software, settings to modify, other software to load and test…the fascination lesson continues to be critical to my livelihood!

With My Kids

I love my kids dearly, and I hope and pray that I am a good father. Mostly, I think I am, but sometimes I find myself getting frustrated by their actions. I know this is something all parents face, but unfortunately, I haven't always handled my frustration in the most productive ways. My approach has, too often, been to raise my voice—both to get their attention and to correct or modify their behavior. While I don't believe there is necessarily anything wrong with this approach; I do believe I use it too often, especially for things that don't require this level of interaction.

This is a behavior I have been working on for some time, and the concept of choosing fascination over frustration (relating to their behavior) is going to be a huge key to helping me change my response.

Frustration and Fascination

We all get frustrated. When things don't go our way; we get frustrated. One of the early lessons we learn as kids is that things don't always go the way you want. Our life experiences have confirmed this. We don't get the promotion, we don't like the way our boss talks to us, our car is making a funny noise, we can't find a parking place, we lose the softball game because of a stupid play by the third baseman, and the list goes on (and on). Our frustrations in life are big and small.

In contrast, to be fascinated is to be captivated by something—to be interested. When we are interested in something, we notice, we observe things. When we are fascinated by something, we are drawn to learn from or about it—quite a different response from frustration, and the places it can lead us.

Choices

So if it is inevitable in life that things don't always go exactly the way we'd like, then typically people would then say it is then inevitable that we will be frustrated. The frustration however, is not the situation itself, but in our response, or choice, to the situation. We have conditioned ourselves to choose frustration. But, we also can choose fascination in these situations. Choosing frustration can lead to regret, anger, resentment and more. Choosing fascination can lead to understanding, knowledge, and improved results and relationships (and more).

The choice is mine. And the choice is yours.

Make your choice wisely.

Better Than a Pot of Gold

When we stay in the present, we remain open to great experiences and amazing opportunities to learn. Stay present; stay in the moment.

I was flying from Los Angeles to Calgary, on my way to give a talk in Kananaskis, Alberta. As we landed, a few minutes late, I reviewed my tasks and did the time calculation. Land, get through customs, get my bag and rent my car. Find a Radio Shack to get the audio items I needed and get on the road for the drive to Kananaskis. I determined that as long as the Radio Shack wasn't too far out of the way, I would have plenty of time for the 90 minute drive. Time to arrive, check in and refresh before the dinner gathering I was expected to attend.

Customs, baggage and getting the rental car went quickly. In fact the kind man at Hertz gave me directions to the store, and it was right on the way! After winding through the mall to the store and getting my items, I checked my watch. I smiled knowing I was on track to have plenty of time for my trip. After all, I had made this drive the previous week—I knew how long it would take to get to my destination in the mountains.

Traffic Tie Ups

On my trip the previous week I had arrived earlier in the day, so I didn't have to go across Calgary in rush hour. My mental plan hadn't taken that *slight* variable into account. And, there was no way I could have known about the road construction that had started over the last few days. Add these two things together, and by the time I passed the site of part of the 1988 Winter Olympics events on the west side of Calgary, my timing was looking tight…

Continuing the Drive

As I left town and continued West, the sun was bright ahead, but it began to rain very hard where I was. With the wipers on high, I thought briefly there probably would be a rainbow somewhere, but I was driving and so, tempted as I was, I kept my eyes on the road. Within a few minutes of driving in the rain, I had forgotten completely about the rainbow possibility as I looked in my rearview mirror. The sky behind me looked funny and strangely colored. I was curious but didn't think much of it.

The Discovery

On my next scan to the mirror, I saw a beautiful rainbow behind me and immediately realized what I had experienced moments before. I had been *in* the rainbow!

Now I drove more with my eyes in the mirror than on the road in front of me. It was a huge rainbow and was getting more brilliant! I love rainbows. I always have. They always have felt magical to me, and I think they are one of the most beautiful things in our world. They also signify for me God's promise that he would never flood the world again.

I continued to spend more than enough time looking in

the mirror as I reviewed my favorite rainbow memories. I quickly realized this moment was at the top of the list. I had been *in* (or very close to) the rainbow! At one point the rainbow seemed to be fading behind one of the large rolling hills behind me, then on my next glance it reappeared in front of that hill.

I reveled in the sight for the next 10–15 minutes and thought about how much I would like a picture of the rainbow. I remembered that I had my digital camera in the trunk. And then I thought about my now increasingly tight time schedule. I wrestled with whether I had the time to stop, find the camera in a bag and get the picture. I wondered if the digital camera would do justice to what I was seeing. Finally, I let go of the excuses and stopped. Forget the schedule, I *had* to capture this moment! I took the pictures. I made the dinner in time (barely). And over the next few days I reflected on (and reveled in) my Canadian rainbow.

Be in the Moment

One of my lessons for this experience was to stay mentally in the moment. I suppose it is possible that I wouldn't have even noticed the rainbow as I drove had I been preoccupied by other things. However, I did struggle with making the time to take the picture because of my schedule.

Two Important Questions

Here is an important question—was I late? No.

And here's a more important question—knowing what I know now, would it have been worth being five minutes late to have that picture and to take just a minute to look at the rainbow with my full attention rather than glimpses in a rear view mirror?

Absolutely.

Next time I am wrestling with staying in the moment, I plan to remember this lesson, and I hope you will too. When we stay in the present, we remain open to great experiences and amazing opportunities to learn. Stay present; stay in the moment.

It's All About Perspective

Rainbows are all about perspective. Where you are compared to the sun and the rain changes the rainbow's location for you. I was in a perfect place at the perfect time to seemingly be in the rainbow. Without the Radio Shack stop, the afternoon commuters and the road work (all things that seemed at the time like nuisances), I likely would not have experienced this unique moment in time. The rainbow seemed to move from behind to in front of the hills as I drove West. It's all about perspective.

The mental and physical places we view things from make a big difference in our perception of those things. It is true for more than rainbows. It is true for your struggles in personal relationships, your business problems, your failures and your successes. When we look at our world from new perspectives we see new things. One of the best things we can do to enhance the quality of our lives is to continue to find new perspectives from which to view our lives.

My work in Kananaskis was fun, and I had the opportunity to spend time with great clients in a wonderful place. But, my trip always will be defined by "my" rainbow.

I wish you rainbows and their lessons.

Short But Not So Sweet

Informed effort is about learning and improvement, about making the right efforts, not just working hard.

The eager employee takes on an assignment to create some reports in Microsoft Excel. He hasn't used the software much, but prides himself on being able to figure things out. Once he clearly understands what the end product needs to look like, he fiddles and tries a variety of things. Once he determines how the task can be completed he works diligently to complete the task. He is proud of his effort and has the task completed in just two days.

The young girl loves basketball, so she shoots baskets. She shoots in the rain; she shoots in the cold. She shoots in the scorching sun; she even shoots in the dark.

The customer encounters a young salesman as he walks in the door. The salesman soon learns that the customer knows what he wants—a certain car among certain colors with some typical options he would prefer not to have. No cars fitting this description are on the lot. The salesman begins what he thinks will be a simple process leading to a sale—find the desired car, get it to the lot and make the sale.

A small search leads to a larger search. A car is found, the paperwork prepared for the sale, only to have the trading dealership sell the car at the last minute. This happens twice. The salesman continues to look, up to 400 miles away, finding only cars that don't match the customer's wants and needs. Eventually, unable to find the car requested, the customer buys the gently used car the salesman recommends.

On the wall of the young salesman's dealership, in big red letters, reads "Effort = Results."

I, as much as anyone I know, love a pithy quote or aphorism. I love quote books, Successories stores and motivational posters. I even publish quotes five days a week read by more than 90,000 people.

But, the saying on the wall at that dealership bothered me. "Effort = Results" implies work hard and you *will* get the result you want. The slogan bothered me because it is wrong, or at least incomplete.

The eager employee completed the job, but with the right information and techniques the job could have been finished in 2 hours rather than 2 days. The budding basketball star will never get on the floor in the game with a shot starting waist high—everyone will block it. And our car salesman worked hard and eventually made a sale, but it wasn't the sale he really wanted to make (and took much longer than he hoped).

Effort isn't always enough. It takes more than hard work.

Informed effort, on the other hand, is a much more worthy goal. We have to know how to use the features and tools of the software, how to correctly shoot under duress, and the intricacies of the car searching process. With this information, the effort put in by our three friends could have been leveraged to much greater success—or they would have reached success with much less effort.

Do you know how to close a sale? How to write a great business letter? How to persuade others to follow your vision? How to make those around you more comfortable? How to let people know you care? How to search the web effectively? How to create more unique ideas and solutions?

Do you know how?

Effort always has been revered in American culture. "She's a hard worker" is one of the best compliments some people would ever give. Don't get me wrong—effort does matter. But if we are putting our efforts in the wrong place, or working without the knowledge of how to do a job easier or more productively, then much of our effort is wasted.

But what about the "results side of this Effort = Results formula?. Effort always will equal results—but not necessarily the results you intend! If you are operating without informed or experienced, then effort alone will lead you *somewhere*, but there is no guarantee it will lead you where you *want* to go.

So how can we turn effort into informed effort?

Here are a few ways—

- Find a mentor
- Get some feedback
- Read about the experts
- Have a coach
- Try a new way
- Attend a workshop or seminar
- Do a web search on your task

Informed effort, in other words, is about learning and improvement, about making the right efforts, not just working hard.

If I could amend the equation on the wall of my car dealer, it would read "Informed Effort = Intended Results." It is probably what the author meant, but it is far from what was said. Are your efforts informed? Are you using your efforts intelligently to help you reach the goals you have set?

Think about this lesson today and make sure your efforts are as informed as possible, but only if you care about your results.

The Great Flood

When we stop to count our blessings rather than focusing on our predicament, our attitude will be able to help us cope with our situation more productively.

We spent the weekend in Michigan, enjoying great weather for the Fourth of July holiday. As we drove the last 100 miles home, it was clear that even though it was sunny, there had been huge amounts of rain during our absence. Corn fields contained lakes, and ditches alongside the road were full of water. We even drove through some very shallow standing water on State Road 29.

We arrived home ready to unpack and relax. A lazy Sunday evening was in my plan, and maybe even going to bed early…I connected my laptop, and thought I would let my email download as we finished unpacking the car. With no mail coming, I knew the cable modem was acting up, so I headed for the basement to investigate.

One step from the bottom, my heart sank, and my priorities changed. The last step was into about 4 inches of water. I yelled, "We have a problem," as I surveyed the extent of the damage. Four inches of water covered the entire finished basement!

I realized quickly that the sump pump wasn't working and the back-up battery powered sump had failed as well. The family mobilized to start moving things upstairs and to the garage. A neighbor joined in to help move things as I got the backup sump pumping again.

Within an hour the bulk of the water had been pumped out, but there was still much "stuff" to be moved up and out. The garage became like triage—we determined what needed to be thrown away, what could be salvaged, what needed to be dried out, etc.

A well-timed call got us priority service for final water extraction and drying. They worked with us to get the basement dry, replace things, get replacement carpet and more.

Our basement is now mostly back to normal. There is new carpet, freshly painted walls, and more plastic storage boxes and less cardboard. Beyond the basic lesson of "No cardboard storage boxes on the floor anymore," we learned much more from this event.

Energy Comes From Action

We had planned a leisurely Sunday evening. We didn't get it. I had driven 300 miles and was a little tired, but after my left foot hit water, I was a whirling dervish until late into the night. We can create energy through action. Dale Carnegie said, "Act enthusiastic, and you'll be enthusiastic." He was right, but there is a larger concept than that. We can act our way into many things, including energy. Energy will arrive when we need it, if we take action.

Attitude Is Important

As neighbors came by and offered to help, they would say how sorry they were. We heard the same thing for several days when the topic would come up. As a family though, we took it as a "temporary inconvenience," and smiled about it. This approach certainly helped our spirits, and also modeled a positive outlook to others. This outlook made our interactions with insurance adjusters, workers and others a much more pleasant experience for everyone.

Kelsey sometimes will cry or whine about some little thing she wants (especially if she didn't get her way). I'll ask her if she likes to cry, and she says no. I'll ask her if crying is going to help her get what she wants in this situation, and she again says no. Then I help her see that the crying is her choice. If crying isn't going to change the outcome, and you don't like crying anyway, why not make a more productive choice?

This was a case where we followed the advice we give our children. Once again we were reminded what a powerful principle this is.

Count Your Blessings

Early Monday morning, when I was trying to dry more papers in the garage, Lori came out and said how lucky we were. Across central Indiana there were many homes "really flooded." We had four inches of relatively clean ground water. Others had 4 feet of, in some cases, much dirtier water. Some people had their main floor flooded, not just their basement.

Our situation wasn't fun and caused much work and a change in our priorities for a couple of weeks. The things we lost mostly could be replaced in kind. We still had a dry place to sleep, no one was injured and everything was going to be fine.

When we stop to count our blessings, rather than focusing on our predicament, our attitude will be able to help us cope with our situation more productively.

There were other lessons learned through the flooding, but

these have had the most impact on me in the months since. I will never wish a flooded basement on anyone, but I will wish you the chance to learn from our experience and apply the lessons we learned.

Energy comes from action.

Attitude is important.

Count your blessings.

Oh, and one more lesson, sump pumps have a 3–5 year life expectancy. Check yours today, and have it tested yearly!

Happy Halloween

Use this as a reminder for the next time you are discouraged. Lift your head up, reflect on what happened, learn from it, smile and go on!

H alloween never has been my favorite holiday. As a kid, growing up on the farm, trick-or-treating meant getting in and out of the car (often on very cold nights) and wearing coats over our costumes. I certainly liked the candy, but it never made much sense to me.

As a father, I must admit I have warmed to the holiday, but I still have a problem with all the focus on witches and ghouls and such. A holiday that focuses on scary things still bothers me just a little bit. I've been pleased that my children have typically chosen more wholesome images to emulate through their costumes.

This year was different though. I've actually been looking forward to Halloween since the middle of June. I planned. I prepared. I thought and strategized about it. But, it didn't go quite the way I expected...

The Garage Sale

Our community has a neighborhood garage sale each June.

By planning everyone's sale on the same day more people attend and the event is more successful for everyone. For several years my son Parker has had a stand selling lemonade, coffee, muffins and cookies, taking advantage of all of the shoppers who came to our cul-de-sac. Last year, my neighbor Jim and I added hot dogs and other grilled food to the menu. People could shop and get a meal too! We had so much fun; we did it again this year.

Only this year, we secretly decided to give the proceeds to our neighbors who have a son with autism. At our annual party, after the sale, we presented them with about $120 (a lot of money when you aren't selling anything for more than a dollar!) to give to the autism group of their choice.

Trying Again

The mix of the fun we had and the response we received from our neighbors led to another idea—let's do this at Halloween. Halloween would be perfect we speculated; lots of traffic (since we always have more than 100 trick or treaters), easy to market (through flyers in the neighborhood), and this year Halloween would be on a Friday. It seemed perfect!

Every few weeks the subject came up. We talked about what to serve and how to market it. Jim, who works in the food brokerage business, got sponsors to provide all the meat. As the calendar turned to October we got more serious and the menu was set: hot dogs, bratwurst, hamburgers and homemade chili.

As I worked on the marketing flyer, all the foods became holiday-themed: Halloweenies, Beastie Brats, Haunted Hamburgers and Chilling Chili. We decided to sell soda and chips. We added a place for kids to bob for apples. We would have the candy from five houses for one stop trick-or-treating. We distributed more than 140 flyers. We were raising money for a great cause. In the final week we even realized we were going to have perfect weather—upper 60's by "game time." We had the perfect setup for a successful event.

Halloween is Here

Friday morning Lori and I made the chili. After lunch we finished shopping for the final items. I couldn't wait to set up! We got everything out—ran extension cords to the street, set up lights, tables and chairs, blocked off the cul-de-sac and fired up the grill.

Two other neighbors were manning the candy—to help the trick-or-treaters get it and to tell them which houses were empty. Parker, age 11, decided to help with the event rather than trick or treat. He would take money and answer questions. Jim would take and fill orders, and I was grill man. We fed the families around us, ourselves and our kids to get the grill going, and they took off to collect candy and good wishes. We were ready.

It got dark, and we had very few trick-or-treaters, and even fewer customers. One mother said she and her son would be back after they were done. We rubbed our hands and prepared for the onslaught.

The onslaught never came.

The Results

By the end of the evening we probably had half our typical number of trick-or-treaters. We sold a little water and soda. We sold a few grilled items. We made $32 (before expenses).

It was a tough night for me. In retrospect, I was as discouraged and disappointed as I can remember being in a long time. It was Sunday before I was really back to normal.

The Lessons

I shook myself out of my self-imposed funk by thinking back on what we did—and what we accomplished. $32. I didn't even count it until Monday. Truth be told, it was more than I expected at that point. My reflection helped me realize that several positive things happened:

- We had fun both planning and doing the event.
- We strengthened neighborhood relationships.
- We taught our children a lesson about caring and doing things for others—through our actions, not our checkbooks.
- We made a memory we will talk about for years.
- We learned what might have to change if we do this again on Halloween!
- I got the subject for this essay.
- A neighborhood shelter got lots of hamburger and hot dog buns.
- And we did add $32 to the Riley Children's Hospital Autism Unit to help them do their work.

However, the best result for me was the lesson of reflection. All the value created by the event was overshadowed in my mind when we didn't reach our goal. My personal goal had been $300. So, in reality, we did about 11% of that goal. I lost sight of all the good by focusing only on the desired outcome.

If you had asked me Saturday morning if the event was a success, I would have grimaced and quickly said no. If you ask me now, I will say that we didn't raise much money, but it was fun, and we learned a lot. Anytime you can have fun while learning is a good experience in my book.

We all suffer defeats, challenges and disappointments. Sometimes they are large; sometimes they aren't. Big or small, I believe there is value and learning in every one of them. Our goal has to be to find those lessons. We only find them by reflecting on the experience and expecting to find them.

Maybe you find yourself reeling from a setback as you read this. If so, please take the message to heart. Maybe the message is more theoretical for you at the moment, that's OK too. Use this as a reminder for the next time you are discouraged. Lift your head up, reflect on what happened, learn from it, smile and go on!

I don't know what next Halloween holds, but we already are talking about the garage sale. We may expand to breakfast. I'll let you know how it goes.

Getting the Right Start

"Stretch your arms,
stretch your legs,
wiggle your toes,
Look up and say,
'Oh what a beautiful day!'"

One night several months ago, without thinking much about it, I got on my knees beside my daughter's bed and, with the help of a couple of her stuffed animals, entertained Kelsey at bedtime. She christened the event a "Show" and suddenly was expecting a "Show" every night as a bedtime routine. I started to add more animals, each with their distinctive (or at least as distinctive as I could make them) voice.

After a couple of weeks, I realized I had created a learning opportunity—Kelsey was remembering the "Show" from the previous night. I decided to seize the learning opportunity to impress on her some important life lessons, just like I try to do here each month (without the stuffed animals).

It was a great learning opportunity for several reasons—she

was truly interested, the timing was good because right before bed is a good time to impress new things in our mind, and I would be able to repeat these messages in future Shows. The first lesson was to help her be less grumpy in the morning.

I put together a little rhyme that I would have Teddy tell her about how to wake up in a more positive way. It went like this:

"Stretch your arms,
stretch your legs,
wiggle your toes,
look up and say,
'Oh what a beautiful day!'"

I repeated the rhyme in my mind a few times to make sure I had it ready for Teddy that night. That Show included several animals discussing how to start the day happily, and why it was important. Then Teddy (the emcee of most Shows) talked about how important it was to begin your day by preparing your mind and body (OK, so I talked about that in the language of four year olds). Then Teddy gave Kelsey his advice, saying: "When you wake up in the morning Miss Kelsey, the first thing to do is:

"Stretch your arms,
stretch your legs,
wiggle your toes,
Look up and say,
'Oh what a beautiful day!'"

Teddy and Kelsey repeated the rhyme until she could

remember it—so it would have a chance to have an impact beyond evening entertainment.

In future Shows Teddy and I added other messages about sharing and kindness and other things that related to what she was learning in her life, but we always reinforced an earlier lesson. And most often, this review included asking Kelsey what she would do first thing when she woke up.

Shows don't happen as often now as they once did. But the lesson of how to wake up is now a part of our lives. If I have the pleasure of waking her in the morning, we do what the poem says while reciting it. And while she can still be a bit grumpy in the morning, I'd like to think the lesson has helped at least a little.

Adult Lessons

The lessons from this story are many, from the ways I helped the learning stick with Kelsey to the truly good advice that is contained in the short poem I composed.

Physiologists tell us we need to stretch our muscles when we first awaken. Our bodies have been inactive for several hours and need to be reinvigorated before we jump up and head into our day. We also know we benefit by putting positive thoughts in our minds first thing in the morning (or at any time during the day for that matter).

I encourage you to think about Kelsey's Show and think about how you start your day. Beyond that, though, I want you to think about how you start:

…your week

…a new project

…a new job

…a new relationship

…and a new year.

We can make choices at the beginning of all of these events to improve our success. We can get off to a better start, with more momentum, greater vitality and excitement—and we can do all of those things by taking time to think about the importance of beginning.

Maybe you will write yourself a checklist, a poem or a prayer. You know what you need to do, if you just take the time to think about it.

Here's to great beginnings.

Give Me a Break!

It is important to remember this doesn't mean focus isn't important; rather, taking breaks support focus because we give our brains and our muscles a chance to refocus on the important task in a productive way.

Parker has worn glasses for several years and has long wanted contacts. During his last eye exam, a few months back, the doctor told him he was old enough to have contacts. He was elated, and I felt helpless. His mother has worn contacts as long as I have known her. The closest thing to corrective lenses I've worn are sunglasses. He had a whole new set of skills to learn—putting in the contacts, taking them out and caring for them.

Over the first few days he got lots of coaching and help from his mother. I would stand and watch, but couldn't be much help—except to provide encouragement. Over time, I hardly thought about it anymore—he seemed to have the task well under control. However, one day recently that temporarily changed.

Parker had finished getting ready for school and I was somewhere else in the house. I hadn't heard him for a few minutes but didn't think much more about it, until I heard a frustrated scream. I rushed to his bathroom and found him very upset. After consoling him, he told me he couldn't get the second contact in; he had been trying for several minutes, but just couldn't get it.

I held him and told him to relax. Then I asked him if it bothered him to walk around with only one contact in. He looked at me warily, as if he was thinking, "Are you going to tell me to go to school with just one contact?" then replied tentatively that it wasn't a problem. So I encouraged him to finish getting ready for school—to take a break from that stubborn right contact.

After some convincing, that is what he did.

A few minutes later, he popped into my office beaming from ear to ear. "When I went back to it Dad, I got it in the first time!" He asked me how I knew that would work (he clearly, and justifiably, doesn't see me as a contact lens expert), and I told him the lesson of "Give Me a Break."

The Lesson

We see this lesson everywhere.

Parker was successful with his contact after walking away for a few minutes then coming back to the task.

Basketball coaches sometimes call a timeout less for tactical reasons than for a chance for the players to catch their breath. Often after the timeout the team plays better, switches the momentum and has more success.

Students working on a test, skip a problem they are stumped by and come back to it later. If they are well prepared for the exam, often on the second try, the solution becomes clear.

We rack our brains trying to solve a vexing business or personal problem. When we set it aside, the solution often will come to us later.

Many times when I'm not traveling I take a quick "power nap" after lunch. These are most effective for me when I enter my 5–10 minute slumber with a specific issue I want to work on when I wake up. Usually, after waking up, my energy level is up *and* the solution I need is clear in my mind.

I could go into all the reasons this lesson works, but that's for another article (or book). The point for us is that it *does* work; whether for crossword puzzles, tough business problems, athletic events, parenting or putting in your contacts.

When hitting a brick wall on your task, take a break. The break may be literal like Parker's, or it may be more mental, like the timeout or closing your eyes and taking a deep breath before continuing your task.

It is important to remember this doesn't mean focus isn't important; rather, taking these sorts of breaks support focus because we give our brains and our muscles a chance to refocus on the important task in a productive way.

As you finish reading think about times when you have applied this lesson, consciously or not. Think about other times when this lesson could have helped you move towards success more rapidly.

In your busy day today, don't be afraid to take a break—the break may be just what you need the most.

Doing a Happy Dance

"Happiness is neither a place nor a fate. Happiness is a way of living."
—*Kevin Eikenberry*

Happiness is something everyone likes and most wish for themselves and others. We comment about people who always seem happy, notice those who always seem to be smiling, and most people seem to "remember the happy times."

When I ask people why they are happy, their answers typically fall into two types of responses. They either say they are generally happy and don't need a reason to be happy, it's just their perspective. Or they say good things have been happening recently making it much easier to be happy.

If you ask generally unhappy people about their mood, you get similar responses. They typically talk about needing a good reason to be happy. They mention life is hard, and—while happiness is a worthy goal—we can't all be happy all the time. However, chances are before giving that perspective, they will share a litany of what is going wrong in their lives, proving of course that you can't be happy with all of that stuff going on.

Something Missing

All that said, in my mind, these responses seem to lack a piece of the happiness puzzle. These responses seem based on genetics and fate. They imply that either I'm a generally happy person (or not) because of my DNA, or that happiness is based entirely on circumstances. If I feel good or if good things are happening to me, I'll be happy, but if I have financial problems, am sick or have other problems, I can't possibly be happy.

Consider Kelsey

I have a beautiful daughter with a generally sunny disposition, but sometimes she gets grumpy—really grumpy. When she gets into her whining act, everything is unfair or not the way she wants it. My common response to this mood is to tickle her, ask her to hug me, or simply ask her to smile. 80% or more of the time doing one of these three actions changes her mood and turns the whines into laughter.

Consider Kevin

Last week I presented at a conference where we also had an exhibit of our products and services. As I greeted people in our booth, I engaged them in conversation. Several people asked me how I was doing and I told them I was great! When asked why, I explained that I had decided it was a good day before I ever woke up. Some smiled and agreed with my approach. Others probably thought it was a rehearsed line to use with people visiting our booth.

It *was* a decision I made when I woke that day. I did things in the morning to reinforce the decision. I walked with a bounce in my step, smiled at everyone I met that morning, opened doors for strangers and whistled a happy tune.

My philosophy always has been that we can decide to look at things positively, and we can act in happy ways. When we do these things, we will be happier. And if things are truly dire, our actions will still leave us feeling better than we would have otherwise.

I've always been proud of my philosophy in this area, but many people have told me things like, "Well Kevin that works for you—you are just naturally a positive, happy person." Clearly they don't buy my philosophy.

Some Proof

Given my philosophy, imagine my happiness when I read about "The Model of Happiness" developed by Dr. Sonja Lyubomirsky and others. This model describes our level of happiness as the sum of three components. They relate closely to what I've already described. The three parts of the happiness model are:

Our Set Point (50%). This is our natural happiness state. We all know people who seem to always be happy, and others who seldom laugh or seem joyful. This gives some (but not complete) credit to the "but you are just a naturally happy person" comment. Stated another way, this model says about half of our happiness can be attributed to this natural inclination.

Circumstances (10%). Our life circumstances also influence our happiness. Things like winning the lottery or spraining an ankle both influence happiness, but typically over a shorter time period. Humans are very adaptable and so major boosts or dips in our happiness are generally short term changes.

Intentional Activity (40%). For this description, let me quote from the Authentic Happiness Coaching Newsletter where I first read of this model:

"The term intentional activities refers to those thoughts and behaviors that require effort. This effort may be apparent only to us (for example, making a list of goals for the week) or it may be visible to others (for example, doing a favor for a friend)....intentional activities are the key to making lasting changes in happiness because such activities are more resistant to adaptation (the process by which we get used to something and become unaffected by it). We can deliberately engage in activities that make us happy while varying them enough to ward off adaptation."

My Conclusions

Other than feeling validated and perhaps a bit smug by this model "proving" my philosophy, I am left with two important observations.

First, most world views on happiness rest with either set point (we are either born happy or not) or circumstances (it's easy for them to be happy, look at what they have going for them). Both of these world views is too limiting and fatalistic.

Second, we *can* actively impact our happiness based on our decisions and actions!

If you want to be happier you can take action to do just that. It is in your control!

There are many actions both large and small that allow us to control this 40% of our happiness. We all know many of them, and you will think of more if you trust yourself.

One of the silly little things I do to maintain or increase my happiness is to do a happy dance. This isn't necessarily a dance I want to share with others (I'm certainly not going to give you a list of my steps) but it is something that makes me happy when I do it. Surprise—my happy dance is one of my "intentional activities".

Sure, "intentional activities" sounds good, but I think "happy dance" sounds better. Don't you?

For You

Examine your own belief system about happiness, and consider incorporating "The Model of Happiness" into your system. Then, make a list of actions you can take to help yourself be happier. However, more important to you than making the list, are the actions you take after making your list.

Note p.s. If you are interested in learning more about the field of "Positive Psychology" consider reading the books of Dr. Martin Seligman, who wrote both *Learned Optimism* and *Authentic Happiness*. His group publishes the newsletter I mentioned in this article. You can learn more at: http://www.authentichappiness.org.

Heads or Tails

If we are more self aware of both our strengths and weaknesses we are better able to manage perceptions—both our own and those of others. We also have a better understanding of those perceptions when they surface.

Several years ago, a friend and I were having a conversation as we walked through downtown San Francisco; I can remember it like it was yesterday. He said, "I can't believe they told me that."

"Told you what?" I asked.

"They said part of the reason they chose the other person is that they felt I was too stubborn. Do you think I'm stubborn, Kevin?"

I paused for a second, looking before we crossed the street, and thought about what I would say next. Rather than answering, I asked some questions. I asked what he felt stubborn meant. My friend replied with a variety of words, phrases and ideas, nearly all of which were stated negatively, or were words and phrases with a negative connotation.

Then I asked my friend to tell me what persistent meant. He gave me another long list of words, framed as positively as the other list had been negative. Just before we came to another street corner, my friend stopped and turned to me.

"I don't know if I'm stubborn Kevin, but I know I am persistent."

After we crossed the street in silence, he said, "They are two sides of the same coin, aren't they?"

I replied, "Often our biggest strengths are also our biggest weaknesses."

I've thought back on this conversation many times. Some recent events have led me to think more about this valuable (and, to me, profound) truth.

I'm not talking about opposite traits (like shy and gregarious); but rather the same trait that plays itself out in different ways or is perceived by others in very different ways.

Some Examples

Here are some examples that cross my mind as I type. They are by no means the only examples, just the ones that come to mind at this moment

- Picky / choosy
- Outgoing / loud
- Funny / a clown
- Strong-willed / opinionated
- Persistent / stubborn
- Cautious / hesitant

Can you see how a trait when viewed in a positive light would be called one thing, and the same one viewed in a different light, or taken to extreme, might be labeled something else?

The Lessons

There are many lessons in this truth, a few of which have been showing up in my life lately.

First, it is important to recognize and play on our strengths. Using our natural strengths allows us to succeed more easily and quickly at most anything. However, when we rely solely on these strengths, they can become weaknesses or liabilities. Think of a fantastic pitcher who has an amazing fastball. If when he gets in a jam he continues to throw only fastballs, bad things can happen. He moves from being overpowering (a good thing in baseball) to "just a fastball pitcher" by over using his strength.

Second, it is important not to obsess about our weaknesses. We need to recognize that weaknesses exist, and yes, if we can improve in those areas, we should go for it. On the other side of the coin, that weakness might be a strength in some way or in another situation. By spending a little time examining "the flipside," we might gain new insight into our own potential.

Third, it is important to manage perception. Some people will perceive our strengths as weaknesses, like in my opening story…others may view one of our weaknesses as one of our biggest strengths. If we are more self aware of both our strengths and weaknesses we are better able to manage the perceptions of ourself and of others. We also have a better understanding of those perceptions when they surface.

Something to Do

If all of this intrigues you, or has given you pause in any way, try the following exercise.

Make a list of your greatest strengths (this is fun). Then get help from someone close to you to find—and list—the negative manifestations of these strengths (this might be less fun).

Having completed these lists will make you more self aware and better able to take advantage of all of the lessons shared above.

I wish you the best with your lists.

What I Learned
on My Trip
to Margaritaville

When we are able to do those four things—use our natural talents, enjoy using them, provide great service to others, and follow our heart and our way—we will have extraordinary joy and satisfaction in our lives.

My story starts five weeks ago when I received Jimmy Buffett concert tickets for my birthday. I've never been to a Buffett concert, and in the weeks since, I've heard lots of stories about what I might experience at the show, heard many references to parrots and have listened to more of his music than I might have otherwise. I also thought about what a phenomenon Jimmy is, and why.

On the way to the concert, Lori and I discussed how few "hits" he's had. We talked about *Come Monday* and *Margaritaville*, and the collaboration with Alan Jackson last year, *It's Five O'Clock Somewhere*.

Other than that, we didn't think he has had many top-40, type hits. She said, "But think of all the songs everyone knows." I agreed. At that point I became even more excited—- I wanted to enjoy the show, but I also wanted to see what I could learn about how Jimmy has become what he has become, without major radio play or hit singles.

After we parked, we sat out a couple of chairs, ate a sandwich and watched the people walk by. I saw more plastic leis and flowered shirts than I have ever seen in my life. I saw huge, plywood fins affixed to the tops of SUVs and in the beds of pickup trucks. The smells of grilling burgers filled my nostrils and the sounds of several familiar Buffett songs filled my ears as we sat and enjoyed the late afternoon sun.

We also met our parking lot neighbors. These folks, about our age, have gone to see Jimmy for many years. They went annually when they lived in Washington D.C., then after leaving DC they flew back every year for the show. Then for several years they traveled to Cincinnati. This was the first year they had come to the Indianapolis show.

We have many of Buffett CDs (well over ten), but these people are *real* fans—they spoke of planning part of a trip to include stopping at a restaurant in Alabama that Jimmy owns with his sister, and mentioned the official Jimmy Buffett magazine. Suddenly my CD collection didn't seem so impressive.

The Concert

Part way through the show Jimmy introduced his next number by saying, "It feels like the start of a vacation. This next song helped me start taking vacations 32 years ago. I would have never dreamed I could still have the chance to do this, and have this much fun, 32 years later. Thank you all." Then he began playing, one of those hits I mentioned earlier, *Come Monday*.

Jimmy Buffett has been selling records for more than thirty

years, but he also is a best selling author, a pilot, a restaurateur and a song writer. He has written the score for a Broadway musical, owned a record company, and who knows what else. And, as I said, he is a cultural phenomenon, and has been for 20 years, with strings of sold out concerts every summer across this country.

Answering My Question

His introduction to *Come Monday* holds many answers to his success. Jimmy Buffett found what he loves, does it well, lets the world see how much fun he has doing it, and invites people to have fun with him. I've never met him, but I really like him. (And I'm clearly not the opnly person that feels that way!) He appeared deeply grateful and fortunate to have the opportunities he has. He was genuine, both then and throughout the show, in his thanks to the crowd for their support. Then he sang a song that tells a great story.

Jimmy Buffett writes songs that are stories, and novels that are like longer songs. Everyone loves stories, and Jimmy tells them expertly. Everyone loves having fun, and Jimmy leads by example. Everyone wants to feel a part of something, and he creates a place where people can belong. If you are at the concert, you are a parrothead, if only for a few hours.

Our Lessons

Don't lose the message of this piece because you think you aren't like Jimmy Buffett—or don't care for his music. He is an extraordinarily talented man, but the lesson is in what he has done with those talents. He has figured out how to use his natural talents, enjoy using them, and bring service to others while doing so. He also has followed his own way, rather than figuring the only way to reach his goals was to do what others did—focus entirely on producing hit records. Listening to and believing in himself lead him to realize his goal—to still be on stage doing what he loves so many years later.

When we are able to do those four things—use our natural talents, enjoy using them, provide great service to others, and follow our heart and our way—we will have extraordinary joy and satisfaction in our lives.

This is my challenge to you. When you accept the challenge to do those four things you will begin the trip to your "stage," to the place where you will shine.

A Lesson in Leadership

If you want to be a leader, take caring action. If you want to develop leaders, encourage people to observe what is needed and to take caring action. If you want to be a more effective leader, get started.

Recently, I spent the weekend at my bi-annual family reunion. About 50 people gathered from several states to celebrate our family connections. We had a good time with wonderful fellowship and some great food.

Since my family and I arrived a day early to help with site and food preparations, I had ample time to do more than just enjoy the event; I had a chance to observe leadership.

Historically, we think about leaders as being those with the most seniority. Churches have elders or deacons, business leaders often skew to the older end of the age demographic, and families have the older generation to take the lead.

Certainly there were those who lead activities and processes at the reunion who were among the older generations, but age or seniority didn't rule completely. In our very loose, non-traditional "organization" leaders stepped forward throughout the event.

We all arrived having received a schedule of events for the weekend's activities. This schedule wasn't like an agenda for a well-planned business meeting with people responsible for every event, but rather a set of ideas and suggestions with times associated with them. We *did*, however, have a solid plan for the meals—everyone in my family likes to eat!

Given that we had this "schedule," but not all the activities had names responsible for them, it was interesting to observe how things happened.

They happened when someone took action…

More people were able to golf because someone recognized that we needed to start some children's activities earlier so more people would be able to go golfing. (Thanks Kerri for noticing, giving up your chance to golf and hanging with the kids until the planned activities began.)

Someone recognized that the hayride the first night was a big hit, so we should keep the tractor and wagons in case people wanted a hayride the second night, even though it wasn't on the schedule. We went again Saturday night with an even bigger crowd. (Thanks Dad for noticing the interest, providing the wagons and driving both nights.)

People pitched in Saturday night to make sure we got the technical glitches solved so everyone could see the collection of family pictures that had been scanned to my laptop. This included unhooking and loading a 32" TV in someone's van, hauling it to the reunion site, and re-installing it so we could make the pictures more easily seen by everyone. (Thanks Joe and David for missing the first wave of dinner to help get this all done.)

Once the bonfire had served its intended purpose—fellowship and s'mores—someone realized the younger kids might prefer to stay there rather than watching the "boring pictures" *and* that the fire really should be tended. So, that person stayed and missed the pictures (that wouldn't have been boring to him). (Thanks Lou for noticing and taking charge.)

These are just a few examples of leadership from my reunion weekend. The lesson for me is that leadership is about personal responsibility and taking action. Without people caring enough to take action, these events either wouldn't have happened or we would have been delayed to the point of effectively losing some of the opportunities we created.

Someone had to tend to the fire.

Someone had to make sure the TV would work.

Someone wanted to give the kids good memories from the event.

*Every*one couldn't do it—some*one* had to step forward. None of the people mentioned were on the reunion planning committee. They found an opportunity to serve and led by their actions.

So it is in your organization. If you want to be a leader, take caring action. If you want to develop leaders, encourage people to observe what is needed and to take caring action. If you want to be a more effective leader, get started.

Worth the Wait

Anticipation can serve us well—providing energy, enthusiasm and a chance to "practice" positive expectancy.

"How many more days, Daddy?" The question became a nightly event over the last week.

"Five days, Kelsey."

"Three days, Kelsey."

"Two more days."

Kelsey couldn't wait until her sixth birthday. She was about to burst with excitement.

A Birthday Deal

She couldn't decide what she wanted for her birthday, so she, her mother and I jointly agreed to let her do something different this year. She was given a certain amount of money to spend at Toy R Us—meaning she got to pick out most of her own presents!

So, on the eve of her birthday, we went shopping. She had a ball picking out her gifts; making some compromises and trades as she juggled the available funds. After getting home, she announced she didn't want to open any of the items yet because it wasn't her birthday. Before the night was over, she changed her mind and opened two, but more were left on the couch as she went to bed.

As she lay in bed she surprised me by saying she couldn't wait to unwrap her presents in the morning! Now, we did have a couple of other small things for her, but she didn't know that—she wanted me to wrap those things that she had picked out earlier in the day. She said, "I'll try to forget what they are so I can be surprised."

The surprise or the anticipation of the event was as important to her as the event or the gifts.

Homecoming is Coming

We have decided to host a tailgate party before the homecoming football game at our alma mater (Go Purdue!) in a few weeks. As we finished an invitation yesterday, Lori said, "I'm getting so excited about this, I'm going to the party supply store to get things for it. And later, I'm going to get online and see what ideas I can get to make this a special event."

The event is six weeks away, and already we are excited about it. Will it be a great time? I'm sure it will be, but even if no one shows up we will have gained much energy and enjoyment just from the anticipation of the event.

A Phone Call

A couple weeks ago we were talking to a veterinarian about our 9-month-old dog. He encouraged us to do several things to make Daxter associate positive things with visitors to our front door. One suggestion was to have a routine that includes having the visitor give him a small treat. The doctor suggested doing this consistently for awhile and eventually Daxter would make ·

the association—and then the treat wouldn't have to be given every time.

In fact, he said, "Anticipation is a powerful thing. Once he is conditioned to expect the treat, he will behave consistently with that expectation even if he doesn't get one every time."

Anticipation

In reflecting on all of these recent events, I keep going back to our veterinarian's comment, "Anticipation is a powerful thing." We all know how powerful it is, but I'm not sure we corral the energy it can provide to us.

Anticipation is the feelings and emotions we gain from thinking positively about future events. Yes, we can experience anxiety or trepidation about future events, and those feelings are anticipatory too, but my examples and focus is on the positive anticipation we feel.

Too often we tie our anticipation to the event that follows; thinking if the event disappoints then our anticipation was futile. Quite the contrary! When we recognize how real the emotions associated with anticipation are we can begin to embrace them and enjoy them more fully, rather than tying them completely to the "results" of the event.

Every football fan loves the anticipation of the game, even if the team loses. Every child is excited about Christmas, regardless of the gifts they receive.

Anticipation can serve us well—providing energy, enthusiasm and a chance to "practice" positive expectancy. Think of the events upcoming in your life and choose to revel in your positive expectations relating to them. We all are good at reveling in great memories, and there is no reason the same can't be true for our positive expectations. Enjoy the events beforehand, as well as during and afterward!

Anticipate joy. Anticipate love. Anticipate success. Do these things and your days will be filled with even more joy, love and success—and whatever else you may anticipate.

Garage Sale Bargains

Part of our role as leaders, parents, and in fact as humans, is to help others reach their potential; to become more valuable and see themselves as more valuable.

W hile pricing items for our upcoming garage sale, Lori asked me, "What should I put on this?" It was a semi-complex, value question. Complex because it involved deciding between what the item is worth vs. the price at which it will sell—and not have to be stored in our house any longer.

Consider Parker's pair of Levi jeans. Buy them full price in a department store and they would be $30. Buy them on sale, as Lori did, and pay $18. Since, for whatever reason, they were barely ever worn even an unbiased person would say they look brand new.

What are they worth…but more importantly, what will they sell for at the garage sale? Someone said, "They are perfect, put $4 on them." Lori agreed as she said, "they are definitely worth that, but will they sell?'

Eventually Lori decided to price the jeans (and many other

items) on the value proposition of "I want them gone!", so she marked them at 50-cents. The jeans sold, but not before one customer asked Lori if she would sell them for a quarter.

This experience left me wondering what is the *real* value of those jeans?

Would they be marked 50-cents in the department store? No, they would sell for $30. If you saw the jeans in the department store for 50-cents would you be skeptical? The first reaction would likely be to look closely for the flaw, stain, tear or bad zipper.

So, does the value we place on an item then change based on the context in which we view it?

Of course it does.

Someone left our garage sale with a loveseat for $40. The seller was thrilled to have the $40. Why? In part, because she didn't want the loveseat anymore! The buyer was thrilled too— thinking, "are you kidding, only $40 for the loveseat?" It reminded me of the oft-repeated phrase, "one man's junk is another man's treasure."

So what is the loveseat worth?

More Than a Garage Sale

People may not be for sale, but we place a value on them in much the same way.

Put the confident young woman with the fiery personality on the debate team and people see an unlimited future for her; perhaps she will be a politician or lawyer. Place that same young woman in a juvenile detection center and we see a different future. Her fiery personality quickly becomes cocky and hot tempered; we might see a life of crime or bad decisions.

How valuable is this young woman?

The employee is always rocking the boat—raising tough questions and not having the answers. No meeting ever ends without this person's input and ideas—lots of them.

The same employee starts a firm—regularly coming up with breakthrough ideas to serve the customers; and encouraging the team to be more creative, take more risks and ask why.

How valuable is this person?

When we change the context in which we view people, we change the perception of their value.

At this point, we cannot take Parker's jeans back to the department store for them to sell—but if we could they would sell for $30.

I can, however, change the way in which I view people and their contributions. I can help people find their own way and place where they can succeed. I can provide people with opportunities to succeed, in part by helping them see the potential that I see in them.

However, to see that potential in others, sometimes I have to let myself see it. In some cases I have to take them out of the mental box or physical location or situation they are in and see them in new ways.

You can do this too.

Part of our role as leaders, parents, and in fact as humans, is to help others reach their potential; to become more valuable and see themselves as more valuable.

We do this by seeing the treasure, not the junk. We do this by not letting people value themselves at garage sale prices.

Look at those you work with, serve with and live with in new ways today. Ask yourself the mental value you are placing on them and decide how accurate you have been. Decide to change your mental projections about these people to Macy's or Marshall Fields', not the second hand store or my garage sale.

Our garage sale netted us a couple hundred dollars, and a few less boxes to store. The lessons I learned about value will last a lifetime.

I hope you got the value, even though you didn't set foot in my garage.

Let's Play!

How many times have you said, "We need to get together for lunch," or "We should go out some time," or "I'll give you a call."?

And how many times have you followed through?

Rich and Lori are pharmacists and had worked together for several years. They always got along great, and they always talked about getting together with some friends and playing euchre—a card game that is especially popular in the Midwestern U.S. Then Rich and his family moved out of town, Lori moved to a different store, and of course talk of euchre was no more.

A few years ago, Rich and his family moved back to town. He and Lori would see each other occasionally at a gathering of pharmacists, and they still had mutual friends. But, in the several years since he moved back to town, they never met socially, even though euchre typically came up when they did chat.

Last December, Lori and I and the kids were shopping at the Target store where Rich works. We visited with him, and when the topic of euchre came up, he looked at me and said, "We are going to do it—we'll call you." I thought there was some resolution in his voice and while we certainly hoped he'd call, I didn't think much more about it.

Until he called, inviting us to play on a Saturday in January.

We arrived at their house as 2 of 16 players. We knew only the hosts and one other couple. While I am a pretty outgoing and social person this was a bit daunting. More than just being there with people I didn't know, the format was that we would each keep track of our own score, rotating partners each game by a process they clearly described.

Then they asked for our $10 each. We were playing for a little cash!

The evening was great fun. We got to meet and play with new and engaging people. We laughed. We ate. And some people even won a little money. As the evening ended I shook Rich's hand and said we would host next.

The event in February at our house was much the same, an eclectic (so eclectic that before the evening started there was no person that had met every other person in the room) group of people coming together to play cards, laugh, and get to know each other.

The March event has come and gone at Rich's home, and dates are being checked for an April gathering back here.

The story of these events isn't really about the cards, although I find that we talk about the games and the players for several days after the parties. The story is that these parties, bringing together former strangers, are creating a new community.

In a typical party, when people from different groups come together, people tend to talk to those they already know, and the integration of "new" people takes time or happens somewhat randomly. Not so with these events. We change partners in every game and usually change tables too; so over the course of the evening most people will have interacted with almost everyone else.

Many great things are happening because of these games. New networks are building and friendships forming or deepening. Memories are being made and lots of laughter is being created. After only three months, the tradition is building—people are expecting and anticipating the next event.

As Martha Stewart says, "It's all good."

It is all good, and it all stems from action taken on a well intentioned social comment. Rich said, "We are going to do it—we'll call you." And then he called. All the benefits I have described have occurred because Rich (and his wife Lynn) got out their calendar and phone list and made some calls.

How many times have you said, "We need to get together for lunch," or "We should go out some time," or "I'll give you a call."?

And how many times have you followed through?

It goes beyond the things you've said, this idea also extends to those intentions you never quite follow through on: sending that thank you note, reading that book on the shelf, learning a foreign language, <insert the one you are thinking about right now here>.

The lesson of the euchre party comes from taking action on the intention. Turning, "I'll call," to "Are you available next Saturday?" Or changing, "That would be fun," to "Let's play."

It's your turn.

What intention have you been thinking about as you have read this, and what action are you going to take...right now?

The Lesson of the Rhubarb Pie

The benefits of greater confidence, the thrill of satisfying your curiosity and the joy of learning often surpass even the experience itself, and nearly always outweigh the risks that come with trying something new.

I love pie, and my Mom makes the best pie crust on the planet. Growing up in west central Michigan we were blessed to have most all of the "pie fruits" grown locally. Early in the season there would be strawberries, followed by raspberries (black and red), then cherries, peaches and apples as the days got shorter again. It was more common than not that pie would be on our dinner table throughout the summer and fall.

Before typical "pie fruits" were in season, there was actually one more type of pie that Mom made—rhubarb. This one was unique because it was the only one I wouldn't eat. All of the others were ultra-yummy, and I my mouth watered when I first stepped into the house to the fresh-baked scent. Rhubarb, on the other hand, was stringy and tart and looked funny. No rhubarb for me, it was the only pie I passed on.

Through much of my kidhood, Jim, who worked with us, joined us for dinner, so with my sister and I that made five at the table. We fit around a round table comfortably, and I have many fond memories of these meals. Pies however are cut into six slices, not five. And before you even mention eight slices, please remember that eight slices makes a piece of pie far too small. That meant there was almost always *one* more slice of pie. This led to many creative ways of determining who got the last piece. This wasn't an issue for the rhubarb though, since I didn't eat it, both Dad and Jim each typically got an extra piece.

One year when Mom made the first rhubarb pie of the spring, Dad and Jim tried to coax me to eat a piece. Coax is probably the wrong word. They teased and cajoled me. They smacked their lips on each bite of their slices, telling me how good it was. Finally, I couldn't take it.

I decided, against my better judgment, to try the rhubarb pie.

I loved it!

As I finished relishing that first piece, my Mom began to laugh at Dad and Jim because she was the first to realize that from now on the games for the sixth piece would include rhubarb pie too. Their attempts to shame me had worked, and it would cost them pie!

That day I was given a love for a new kind of pie and a lesson I haven't yet forgotten—you never know until you try.

Growing up I was a picky eater, and even today I'm not the most adventurous in trying new foods. While I am sure the rhubarb lesson helped to loosen up this pickiness a little, there are still many things I don't like the taste of. But I have, for the most part, at least now tried them.

In other areas of my life though, I think I have followed the advice of "try it, you never know until you try" consistently and with great success.

You Never Know

Before you try something—whether it is skiing, a new problem solving technique, a new book or rhubarb pie—you might think you know what it is like. You might have read about it, heard about it, thought about it or dreamt about it. Regardless, nothing can replace the experience of trying it. Until you try, you can't know what that snow feels like under your skis. You can't explain the "aha" that the technique brings. You can't describe how the story makes you feel, and you can't taste the sweet tartness of the rhubarb.

You've got to try it.

If it is something you have thought about at all, you surely will have opinions formed about it. Those opinions—not the real experience—may be why you have avoided trying up until now.

Do what you can to banish those opinions. Try with an open mind.

You've got to try it.

This insight and advice can apply to little things, like the routine you use to mow your lawn (which is what I was thinking about that led to this essay) and to big things in your personal or professional life.

Never played a musical instrument? Try it.

Never been to a networking event? Try it.

Never been to a church of a different denomination? Try it.

Never done your banking online? Try it.

Never played racquetball? Try it.

Never learned a foreign language? Try it.

The benefits of greater confidence, the thrill of satisfying your curiosity and the joy of learning often surpass even the experience itself, and nearly always outweigh the risks that come with trying something new.

Find at least one thing today, large or small, to try. And if you haven't had a piece of rhubarb pie, that might be a good place to start.

They've Got Game

*We don't have to do it alone. We can reach our goals faster—
and have more fun—when we find people to collaborate with
us—whether it is on a new business venture, a church event, or
learning a video game.*

I am the father of a 13-year-old boy, which means, I have a
son who is a fan of video games. I stood in line the day
after Thanksgiving several years ago to get him his first
GameBoy. (He wanted the Yellow Poke'mon one). When
he wanted a Playstation2, we worked out an arrangement where
he could earn one, which he did. Since these events, each birthday and Christmas wish list has included games for one of his
gaming devices.

Birthday parties and sleepovers at our house don't typically
find Parker and his buddies outside playing baseball or riding
bikes or doing the things I might have done at their age. Rather,
I can walk to the basement and find a gaggle of guys looking at
the television screen—watching one player play a particular
game.

For many years I found this to be so unusual. My sense of
play, and my sense of competitiveness, made this behavior hard
to understand or explain. I've always wondered why they would
want to be so passive. Sometimes three or four would watch

another play a game, even when the game allowed two players! It seemed so boring to those not playing.

This summer one of Parker's good friends, Kendall, has spent a couple of days at our house. Some of the same game behaviors have persisted, but, on closer observation, I have found something more. Parker has a new game that allows a two player mode that doesn't have people pitted against each other, but rather, they can work together as partners to reach the game's objectives. Not once have I seen (or heard) them playing this game solo, with the other person watching.

A few weeks ago Parker wanted to use some of his money to buy a new game for his GameBoy. A couple of days after Parker's purchase (and immediate immersion into it—as much time as we allowed), Kendall purchased the same game.

Since that time, nearly every day there has been a phone call between them. The main topic of conversation is their progress in this complex game. When they are together now, they play this game together, with Kendall's cord that connects their two handheld units. They exchange codes and secrets to help each other advance. They might comment on who has made more progress to completing the game, but that clearly isn't their focus. Their focus is collaborating so they can both succeed.

Like Son, Like Father?

Many of you reading this know that I consult with and train organizations to have more effective teams. I believe in the synergy that comes from people working effectively together. Even beyond the structure of formal teams, the power of collaboration can not be overstated.

There really is no such thing as a self-made person. Every success in every walk of life has had a partner, a confidant, a mentor—someone or ones that have helped that person achieve their goals.

After all, where is Bill Gates in business without Paul Allen?

Or Stan Laurel in entertainment without Oliver Hardy?

And for that matter, where is Parker Eikenberry in Mega-Man 5 without Kendall Witty?

When we become mature enough, and smart enough, and even confident and self assured enough, we are ready to open ourselves up to collaborating with others.

We don't have to do it alone. We can reach our goals faster—and have more fun—when we find people to collaborate with us—whether it is on a new business venture, a church event, or learning a video game.

I've begun to re-assess my observations of Parker and his buddies playing video games. As a parent, I used to think it rude if Parker was playing while the others were watching. Now I know that is likely *not* the case. Instead, what I am witnessing in my basement is collaboration. Four sets of eyes watching one player. As they watch they are certainly learning how to succeed better themselves on their turn, but they also are offering coaching and advice at all times.

One person playing, the others supporting the player. And the roles switch easily and seamlessly.

So it can be with us. We can choose to collaborate more easily. We can choose our time to play and our time to support. And in the end, in taking these steps, we will reach our goal more quickly. Just like Parker and Kendall will complete Mega-Man 5 more quickly using an approach that came naturally to them.

Lessons of the First 100

Too many of us on too many days, move from morning to night, from meeting to meeting or task to task, completing the routine of life as if it is only that; a routine.

This is the 100th Vantagepoints essay I will write and publish. It also is the last essay in this book. In preparing to write this essay, and in preparing the book for publication, I have read the other 99 essays in a relatively short period of time. One would hope that this 100th essay would be significantly better than the first one I wrote.

I mean, if I shoot 100 free throws, or repeat the Gettysburg Address 100 times, or practice saying Happy Birthday in French 100 times, I would expect to be better at those things at the end of the repetitions than when I started.

I believe that this is true of my writing. I *am* a better writer now than when I started (whew!).

Beyond the individual lessons I have written about in each essay, there are other things I have learned through this writing journey, and it seems fitting to share them with you. I don't share them to gloat, as in "see what I've learned." I share them because I believe you can learn from my lessons (which is part of what *Vantagepoints* is about), and I share them because in reflecting on and writing about them, the lessons become more a part of me (which is another part of what *Vantagepoints* is about).

Everyday

The subtitle of this book is "Finding Learning Opportunities in Everyday Life Situations." I have learned that there are lessons for us everyday. In order to find those lessons, we must expect them, which demands that we keep our eyes, ears and minds open for them. Too many of us on too many days, move from morning to night, from meeting to meeting or task to task, completing the routine of life as if it is only that; a routine.

Like the parent who asks their children at the end of a school day, "What did you learn today?", we must ask ourselves this question. We expect learning opportunities for the kids each day—that is why they are in school after all. It is the same for us. As human learning beings, the reason we live each day is in part to learn.

I have found that the opportunities for us to learn are all around us in both the unique experiences and in the normal route we drive each morning or the way we make our coffee.

The lessons are waiting for us around every corner and in every conversation. Everyday.

Reflection

While looking for the lessons is a necessary first step, it isn't enough. We must take time to reflect on those experiences. Without open eyes and ears we don't have experiences to reflect on, but without time to analyze and think about those experiences, we won't harvest the rich lessons available to us.

A military unit debriefs after a mission. A sports team watches the game film. A skilled trainer asks people a well developed series of questions after any learning experience. Why? Because they know that by reviewing the experience, there is a chance to learn from that experience, gain more knowledge from it, and be more successful or productive in the future.

This is what we must do. We must reflect on our experiences in order to gain the most from them.

Writing 100 of these essays has forced me to reflect—after all, I needed to find something to write about each month. What I have learned over the years though is that reflection, like any other skill, develops with practice.

In the quiet moments of your day, think about your recent experiences. Ask yourself what went well, how you were surprised, and what was different. Ask yourself how those experiences relate to other recent experiences and what you can learn from the combinations. Then ask the most important question—what will you *do differently* with your new knowledge and understanding.

Retelling Stories

Stories are powerful ways to share a message. That is why we watch movies and read novels. That is why the stories I tell during a speech are among the most powerful things I can do. Hearing or reading someone else's story can be very useful. It can engage us, prompt us, and teach us.

But this isn't my lesson.

Yes, stories are powerful. But the most powerful stories are the stories *we* tell. In telling our stories we are reflecting on our lessons. By telling our stories we understand them better than we did before we told them.

It is what I have now done 100 times. Experienced something(s), reflected on the experience, found some lessons, and told the story. Each link in this learning chain is helpful, but the telling of the story completes the loop. There are many experiences that lead to the seed of a *Vantagepoints* essay. They typically make a lot of sense in my head, but until I tell them (in my case write them) the lessons often are vague and disconnected.

Something magical happens when we talk or write about a concept—we begin to solidify our understanding and truly make sense of what has been in our heads.

I have learned that stories aren't just powerful to read or hear, they are powerful to tell.

Action

The theme and lesson that comes through most of these essays is "take action." Nothing happens until we take action.

I have ended each essay by encouraging you to do something. Through my example, I hope you have taken my advice (more than once). But I can't take the action for you.

There are two things I know for sure. You maximize the value of what you learn by putting it into action. And no one can do that for you.

Your lessons await you, and I urge you to discover them. Take the time to think through your experiences and create stories to help you make the learning more concrete and real. Most of all, take what you have learned and put it into action.

When I do those things I am most successful.

When you do those things you will be most successful too.

Life is happening all around you. The learning awaits.

About Kevin Eikenberry

Kevin Eikenberry is an expert in developing organizational and individual potential who lives with his family in Indianapolis, Indiana. Kevin holds a B.S. with honors from Purdue University. He is a motivating and inspiring speaker and a dynamic trainer and consultant. Kevin's students and clients consistently rave about his effectiveness, many calling him "the best trainer I've ever experienced."

As the Chief Potential Officer of **The Kevin Eikenberry Group**, Kevin and his team provide a wide range of services, including training delivery and design, facilitation, performance coaching, organizational consulting and speaking services. Kevin has spent the last 12 years helping organizations all across North America reach their potential.

As a speaker, Kevin gives keynotes for organizations and non-profit groups on life-long learning, developing human potential, leadership, teams and teamwork, creativity and more.

Kevin is a contributing author of the best-selling book *Walking with the Wise* (Mentors Press 2003), and has been a contributor to ten Training and Development Sourcebooks since 1997. He also is a contributor to Pfeiffer and Company's *20 Active Training Programs, Volume 2*. He publishes three electronic publications, in addition to *Vantagepoints*, one of which is read by more than 90,000 people worldwide. His articles have been published in more than 50 Internet newsletters and featured on many websites. Kevin also has been recognized in *Who's Who in the Midwest* and *Who's Who Worldwide*.

For more information about Kevin or his training, speaking or consulting services, please contact:

The Kevin Eikenberry Group
7035 Bluffridge Way * Indianapolis, IN 46278
phone: (317) 387-1424 * fax: (317) 387-1921
Vantagepoints@KevinEikenberry.com
KevinEikenberry.com
Vantagepoints.net

Our Special Thanks to You

I am so pleased that you have purchased and read this book! As a way to show my appreciation, we have packaged some of our products and also persuaded many friends and colleagues—experts, trainers, authors and coaches—to provide you with some of their best resources and tools to further support your lifelong learning journey.

This vast collection of resources and tools are my thank you gift to you.

You can view, learn about and take advantage of all of these resources by going to http://vanatagepoints.net/resources.asp.

Thanks again, and I wish you great success on your learning journey.

Yours in Learning,

Listen to *Vantagepoints* Live

Kevin is available for a limited number of speaking engagements. Hire him for your next meeting, conference or convention to inspire, inform and engage your audience!

In this inspiring story-filled keynote, Kevin turns the concept of lifelong learning into something real that everyone can apply each day.

Kevin Eikenberry is an expert in developing organizational and individual potential and the Chief Potential Officer of **The Kevin Eikenberry Group**. Through his own experience, study, and creating learning events for organizations across North America for the last 15 years he has developed a unique perspective into how we can transform our life events into meaningful learning.

This keynote, based this book, is energizing and inspiring and practical with specific ideas people can apply immediately. After listening to Kevin's speech, **Vantagepoints on Learning and Life—Finding Learning Opportunities in Everyday Life Situations,** your audience will be on its way to seeing life experiences from a new vantagepoint.

Contact us about this or other keynote programs at 317.387.1424 (or 888.LEARNER toll free in the U.S.) or info@KevinEikenberry.com.

THE
KEVIN EIKENBERRY
GROUP

How We Help

If you have just finished reading any portion of this book we
hope you are clear about Kevin's belief in learning. He runs his
business based on his personal philosophy that we are at our best
and achieve our best results when we are learning. All of our
products and services support this philosophy—to help you as a
continuous learner achieve success at the highest level.

Wow Your Audience with Kevin as Your Speaker. Kevin has
delivered keynote speeches and training across the United States
and Canada, presenting to small intimate groups and to audi-
ences of 1,000 or more (and all sizes in between). His presenta-
tions give you inspired solutions, relevant approaches and
interactive fun. Visit www.KevinEikenberry.com/speaking.asp to
learn why Kevin should speak at your next meeting, conference
or convention!

*"His dynamic presence and presentation both energized and
informed the group. People left not only more knowledgeable, but
more importantly, believing in themselves. They were clearly going
to try out what they had learned."*
—*Chris Saeger, Manager of Program Development, American Red
Cross*

**Learning that Lasts—Effective Training Customized to Meet
Your Needs.** Whatever you call it—training, a class, a workshop
or a seminar—we can deliver it! You will receive a customized

training plan to meet your specific needs to provide learning that lasts. Training with us leads to powerful results: improved skills, increased productivity, loyal employees and delighted Customers. Discover the different training services we offer at www.KevinEikenberry.com/training.asp.

"I felt the training was well worth the expense. At first I thought it might be far too expensive, but I was impressed with the material, the presentation format, the message and the results. Kevin is, by far, the best example of a training professional I have ever seen."

—Mark E. David, Program Manager, Allison Engine Company

Helping Your Organization Succeed with Our Consulting Services. Whether you are looking for coaching, Customer service, facilitation, instructional design, organizational change, strategic planning or team building our consulting services provide real change, empowered organizations, productive teams and greater business success. Learn how we can help you succeed at www.KevinEikenberry.com/consulting.asp.

"Kevin has a high degree of integrity. I can count on him to tell me the truth about my plans, the ability of my organization to implement those plans, and the role I need to be playing to reach my objectives. He even tells me when I don't need his services…it doesn't get any better than that. It's a great package, and it works for me."

—Joan Posluszny, Manager Human Resources Service Center, Chevron Corporation

Leadership Development. The best and most successful leaders believe in the power of continuous learning. We offer a wide variety of delivery methods for our leadership products including tele-seminars, learning systems, downloadable MP3 recordings and audio CDs to cater to different learning styles. All our products are designed to help you on your journey to becoming a remarkable leader! Visit www.KevinEikenberry.com/products/leadership.asp to learn more.

"Excellent tele-seminar. I especially liked the handouts you provided in advance and the follow-up e-mail information. You delivered real-life, practical advice in a user-friendly way. What you did will help leaders from many arenas grow in their ability to effectively manage change in their organizations."
—*Guy Harris, Recovering Engineer & Leadership/Executive Coach*

Unleash Learning. You already know by reading this book that we have a strong belief in continuous learning. The products we've developed exist to help you on your journey of learning. We offer products in a variety of topics including creativity, consulting, leadership, general learning, teamwork and training. Visit http://KevinEikenberry.com/products/index.asp often as we are always adding and developing new products to help you unleash *your* potential.

"Kevin's products not only provided valuable information on how I could become a greater asset to my company, but he also gave me the tools I needed to manage my own career satisfaction. That, in itself, will remain of value to me for years to come."
—*Donna Ward, HR Director, Ide Management Group*

Complimentary Resources from The Kevin Eikenberry Group to Help You, Your Team and Organization Grow!

Here you will find a variety of resources to help you keep learning! Take the time to visit the links, search for your interests and take advantage of our free learning opportunities.

Vantagepoints. A monthly story similar to those in this book delivered via email. Vantagepoints will inspire you to see that your daily situations are opportunities to learn and grow.

> *"Stories capture our imagination; great stories can contribute to our learning and personal growth. Kevin's stories and comments help us see great truths and become better people."*
> *—David R.*

Visit www.Vantagepoints.net to sign up for this free, monthly message!

Unleash Your Potential with Kevin Eikenberry. This free e-zine is designed to help you achieve professional and organizational success. Each week you will find it full of ideas, tools and resources to help you do what the title says, "Unleash Your Potential."

> *"Your newsletter is the only one I read in its entirety, and I always get some great information. It is timely, educational, up-to-date and well written! I also save them as a future source of information."*
> *—Hazel Walker, Executive Director, BNI—Indiana Chapter*

Subscribe at www.kevineikenberry.com/uypw and receive a FREE Special Report on potential!

Kevin's Blog. Kevin writes in his blog several times a week to provide you with resources, techniques and ideas (and some other interesting stuff) to help you reach your professional potential. You can subscribe to updates via email, through your RSS reader, or visit the site often.

Visit www.kevineikenberry.com/blogs/index.asp to get connected and check out past postings.

Powerquotes. Read by more than 100,000 people worldwide each week, Powerquotes features an inspiring quotation with questions to reflect on. Delivered every Monday, this free e-zine will give a positive start to your week.

"Your service is by far the best quote service out there. Keep those quotes coming and keep up the good work!"
—Jolene S

Sign up at www.powerquotes.net!

Articles to Unleash Your Potential. You will find an archive of more than 75 articles on a variety of topics and skills. They are a good resource for improving your results personally, plus you can reprint the articles for your website or newsletter.

Review the archives at
www.kevineikenberry.com/resources/articles.asp.

To Order More Copies Of

Vantagepoints on Learning and Life—

Finding Learning Opportunities in Everyday Life Opportunities

$16.95

Visit www.Vantagepoints.net

CALL 1-888-LEARNER / (317) 387-1424

OR

AVAILABLE AT BOOKSTORES EVERYWHERE

Contact us for Quantity Discounts.

Visa/MasterCard/American Express

Printed in the United States
47027LVS00001B/19-64